KU-241-905

THE

PRIMAL
KITCHEN
COOKBOOK

Eat Like Your Life Depends On It!

131 of Mark's Favorite Recipes (Low Carb, Gluten Free)
Hand-Picked from 50+ Top Paleo Authors and Chefs

MARK SISSON

PRIMAL
BLUEPRINT
PUBLISHING

The Primal Blueprint Cookbook: Eat Like Your Life Depends On It!
Copyright © 2017 Mark Sisson. All rights reserved.

Except as permitted under the United States Copyright Act of 1976, reproduction or utilization of this work in any form or by any electronic, mechanical, or other means, now known or hereafter invented, including xerography, photocopying, and recording, and in any information storage and retrieval system, is forbidden without written permission of the publisher.

Mention of specific companies, organizations, or authorities in this book does not imply endorsement by the author or publisher. Information in this book was accurate at the time researched. The author received no incentives or compensation to include the recipes from outside contributors to this book.

Library of Congress Cataloging in Publication Control Number: 2017007987
ISBN: 978-1-939563-36-1

Editor: Leslie Klenke
Cover Design: Janée Meadows
Interior Design: Janée Meadows
Interior Design & Layout: Julie Schauer
Photography: Janée Meadows
Food Styling: Leslie Klenke & Janée Meadows
Copy Editor: Amy Lucas
Proofreader: Tim Tate
Index: Tim Tate
Recipes: Contributors listed on pages 309–321

Primal Blueprint Publishing, 1641 S. Rose Ave., Oxnard, CA 93033. 888-774-6259. info@primalblueprintpublishing.com. PrimalBlueprintPublishing.com. Please contact the publisher with any questions, concerns, and feedback, or to obtain quantity discounts.

DISCLAIMER: The ideas, concepts, and opinions expressed in this book are intended to be used for educational purposes only. This book is sold with the understanding that the author and publisher are not rendering medical advice of any kind, nor is this book intended to replace medical advice, nor to diagnose, prescribe, or treat any disease, condition, illness, or injury. It is imperative that before beginning any diet, exercise, recipes, or lifestyle program, including any aspect of the methodologies mentioned in *The Primal Blueprint Cookbook* and the Primal Blueprint lifestyle in general, you receive full medical clearance from a licensed physician. If you are currently taking medication for health conditions, are pregnant or a growing youth, or have a current or past condition such as cardiovascular disease, cancer, diabetes, or other serious health condition, major dietary changes should be considered with extreme caution and the guidance of a trusted medical professional. The author and publisher claim no responsibility to any person or entity for any liability, loss, or damage caused or alleged to be caused directly or indirectly as a result of the use, application, or interpretation of the material in this book. If you object to this disclaimer, you may return the book to publisher for a full refund.

Whole30 is a registered trademark of Thirty & Co., LLC, and was used in this book with permission.

Printed in the U.S.A.

WELCOME
from MARK 1

AIP Autoimmune Protocol

DF Dairy Free

K Ketogenic

NAS No Added Sugar

V Vegan

W30 Whole30®

SAUCES
and DRESSINGS 11

SMOOTHIES
and BREAKFASTS . . . 49

MAIN DISHES 213

DESSERTS 263

CONTRIBUTORS . . 309
INDEX 323

AIP Autoimmune Protocol

DF Dairy Free

K Ketogenic

NAS No Added Sugar

V Vegan

W30 Whole30®

WELCOME
from MARK

Thanks for joining me on my journey of living awesome and enjoying food as one of the great pleasures of life. This cookbook is a special effort to blend a couple of my passions: researching and writing about primal living, and designing healthy pantry staples. Nearly a decade ago, I wrote and self-published a book called *The Primal Blueprint*, detailing ten diet, exercise and lifestyle laws patterned after our hunter-gatherer ancestors that promote optimal gene expression. By adapting the ancient, evolutionary-tested laws into the realities of high-tech modern life, you can easily reduce excess body fat, increase energy and vitality, and promote longevity instead of the accelerated aging and disease epidemics we see today.

At first, my message was not welcomed by the establishment. No publisher wanted to take a chance on the book. "You're not a doctor, Mark." "You need a major celebrity attached, Mark." "Exercise less, eat more fat, and lose weight? That's crazy, Mark!" Respected health authorities viciously attacked the counterculture ideas advanced by the burgeoning ancestral health movement. Fortunately, user experiences started to mount, and the primal/paleo movement of eating and living could no longer be discounted. Take a look at the thousands of success stories on MarksDailyApple.com, or the massive explosion of all things paleo on the shelves of mainstream book and grocery stores. When people ask me if primal/paleo is a fad, I remind them that this "fad" is 2.5 million years old! While not all doctors and nutritionists agree with the core principles of primal eating such as the need to avoid grains, or that saturated fat is healthy to eat, the tide is finally turning. Even the mainstream medical establishment is now validating that chronically excessive insulin production driven by a grain-based diet is the predominant public health crisis of modern times.

Getting Granular About Primal Eating

The recipes in this cookbook have incredible nutrient density and variety, provide high levels of satiety, and are devoid of the most health-compromising agents in our modern food supply—namely refined sugars, grains, and vegetable oils. By comparison to the Standard American Diet (SAD), primal recipes are high in fat, low to moderate in protein, and very low in carbohydrate. They are all grain free, and consequently gluten free.

This is indeed a radical departure from a diet, or cookbook, which emphasizes food like wheat, rice, corn, pasta, and cereal. But the primal/paleo eating style is exactly what enabled our *Homo sapien* ancestors to thrive in survival of the fittest conditions. Today, since we are genetically identical to our ancestors 10,000 years ago, optimal gene expression is achieved when we model the diet and lifestyle practices of our pre-civilized ancestors. When you eat primally, you are able to escape from the carbohydrate dependency caused by SAD eating patterns and become what I like to call a *fat-burning beast*. If you are reliant upon regular meals for energy and concentration, or have struggled to lose excess body fat despite eating sensible portions and exercising diligently, or you have health conditions like gluten sensitivity, leaky gut syndrome, autoimmunity, or chronic inflammation, escaping carb dependency and becoming a fat-burning beast could be the greatest health awakening of your life.

Lest you misinterpret the primal approach as anti-carb, let me clarify that there is nothing wrong with enjoying nutrient-dense carbohydrates, and that Primal Blueprint guidelines allow for an average of 150 grams (400 calories) of carbohydrate intake daily. This affords an abundant intake of vegetables (indeed, they should be the centerpiece of your diet, as everyone agrees). It also includes a sensible intake of seasonal fruits and other nutritious carbs like sweet potatoes, quinoa, and wild rice, along with incidental carbs from nuts, seeds, high cacao percentage dark chocolate, and some occasional light sweetening of beverages, such as adding honey or maple syrup to wholesome recipes.

I'm not anti-carb, but I'm definitely anti-grains and anti-gluten! I call grains *beige glop*—a cheap source of calories that are immediately converted to glucose upon ingestion, offer minimal nutritional value, and which likely cause mild-to-serious issues in almost everyone due to the presence of anti-nutrients, such as gluten. Gluten trashed my body for decades without me even being aware of it, and science validates the idea that there is no health justification for humans to ever consume grains.

Besides, grains themselves are bland-tasting; it's the *stuff you put on them* that have made grains a cultural dietary centerpiece for thousands of years that you think you can't live without, (unless you're telling me you can't live without a steaming bowl of plain white rice or pasta noodles). If you purchased this book looking for 101 ways to make rice or pasta come alive, sorry to disappoint. If you start consuming, delicious, deeply satisfying, wholesome primal recipes, you may be surprised how quickly you can completely transition away from grain-based meals—even your all-time favorites—in a very short time.

The Advent of Primal Kitchen

Frustration has been brewing for years in the primal/paleo community that it's tough to find healthy alternatives to mainstream brands of sauces, dressings, and condiments. My breaking point came one day in late 2014. While making my beloved tuna salad, (see the YouTube video I shot years ago called, "Big Ass Salad"), I cringed once again when I was obligated to throw a tablespoon of oxidized vegetable oil into my masterpiece. As soon as I commenced R&D for our first Primal Kitchen product, the Classic Mayo (first released in February of 2015), I realized that it was not only possible to create mayo with impeccable ingredient standards, but that it also tasted better—a ton better!—than the highly refined crap we've been choking down our entire lives. Alas, ambitious undertakings like popping for a minimum initial production run of 12,000 jars, and then going after the big boys in Big Food is nerve-wracking to say the least. (Can you say, "bribery for eye-level shelf space?" I can't... .) But the resounding consumer response, right out of the gate, leaves everyone at Primal Kitchen forever indebted to the community of health-conscious consumers who are demanding something better.

This cookbook is an effort to express my appreciation for everyone involved in the real food movement. I'm grateful to distribution partners like Whole Foods Market, Thrive Market, and countless small independent grocery stores for taking a chance on a small-time operation out of Oxnard, California. Your involvement as a consumer in search of healthier products, has made a tremendous impact on the food and nutrition industry.

This appreciation extends to how we run our business and quality-control our products. We adhere, uncompromisingly, to narrowly-defined specifications. We use only the healthiest, freshest fats and oils. In addition to our mayos and dressings, we've partnered with California farmers to present fresh, first cold-pressed only, emerald green extra-virgin avocado oil in stand-alone bottles. We source the most potent phytonutrient and superfood agents, and have zero tolerance for the all-too-common offensive ingredients found in the easy and inexpensive-to-manufacture offerings from the major food conglomerates.

Our mission statement has made product development and price competition extremely difficult. In some cases, we purchase materials that cost 20 to 40 times more than materials used in conventional products. Our commitment to using only the most nutritious oils is a far cry from your favorite celebrity-endorsed salad dressings made with "olive oil blends" (that are typically diluted with cheaper-grade oils for cost savings), or "soybean oil and/or canola oil," both of which have the potential to generate oxidative stress immediately upon ingestion.

Why Avocado Oil?

Many experts assert that avocado oil may just be the healthiest and most versatile of all oils. For example, the *Journal of Nutrition* published a study showing that salads dressed with avocado oil delivered 15 times more carotenoids than those without. Avocado oil, the foundation for each Primal Kitchen mayonnaise and salad dressing, is high in monounsaturated fatty acids. Monos, lauded universally as "heart-healthy" fats, are full of immune-boosting polyphenols and phytonutrients.

Avocado oil lacks the inflammatory properties of so many other oils, particularly the highly refined polyunsaturated vegetable/seed oils found in most condiments and processed or frozen foods. Oils like canola, soybean, corn, safflower, sunflower, and the like sustain oxidative damage during their high-temperature processings, and are vulnerable to damage from heat, light, and oxygen. Heating these oils, for pan frying and such, is especially objectionable. Instead it's recommended to use saturated animal fats (such as butter, lard or bacon grease), or highly saturated, temperature-stable plant products like coconut oil or avocado oil. Avocado oil's pleasant, but not overpowering, taste also makes it a great choice on vegetables and salads, or for use in homemade salad dressings.

In contrast, refined high polyunsaturated oils are perhaps the most health-offensive food you can consume, as it has been demonstrated that they might contribute to disturbances in healthy cellular function at the DNA level. Dr. Cate Shanahan, family physician, author of *Deep Nutrition* and Nutrition Director for the Los Angeles Lakers, explains how polyunsaturated oils are essentially "free radicals in a bottle." They are integrated into cell membranes after ingestion, and become difficult to burn off, due to the unnatural molecular structure caused by high temperature processing. They can help promote systemic inflammation, inflict oxidative damage immediately upon ingestion, accelerate aging, hamper immune and cardiovascular function, severely compromise your ability to remove excess body fat, and may be linked to assorted cancers. When you are eating salad at a restaurant (believe it or not, even the finest restaurants) or tuna salad at a deli, you can be certain that they were made with refined vegetable oils. The next time you dine out, consider Dr. Cate's scientifically-validated quip that consuming vegetable oils is, "literally no different than eating radiation." Instead, consider taking your own salad dressing into the restaurant or the breakroom at work. Don't worry, it's allowed—I checked!

How to Use This Book

Contributors

As you learned earlier, I'm not a doctor, nor am I a gourmet chef. While I consider myself an expert on health and nutrition, perhaps my most relevant credential for writing my cookbooks is that I'm a guy who loves to eat. For this project, I solicited contributions from some of the most popular and respected chefs and health authorities in the "paleosphere." At the top of every recipe page, you'll see either the contributor's name, my name (if it came out of my home kitchen), or Primal Kitchen, if it's a homemade preparation modeling one of our commercial salad dressings or mayos. There is a full biography section starting on page 309, so you can learn more about the contributors and how to connect with them.

Aligning with Your Dietary Goals

The next section discusses special icons that designate how each recipe might align with your distinct dietary goals. While you won't see a symbol for grain free or gluten free anywhere except on the front cover, all of the recipes presented are completely grain free and, therefore, also gluten free.

Recipe Icons

At the top of every recipe, you'll see an icon bar to help you determine which recipes align with your specific dietary goals. The icons are: AIP, DAIRY FREE, KETO, NO ADDED SUGAR, VEGAN, and WHOLE30. The following is a brief breakdown of what each icon means:

 AIP
Autoimmune Protocol restricts foods believed to cause leaky gut and systemic inflammation in sensitive people, including: eggs, grains, dairy, legumes, nuts, seeds (including spices derived from seeds), nightshades (tomato, eggplant, etc.; including spices derived from nightshades), sugars and sweeteners, alcohol, and all processed foods, oils, and chemical additives. Additional details can be found at **aiplifestyle.com** or **thepaleomom.com**.

 DAIRY FREE
Free of all dairy (milk, cheese, cream cheese, cottage cheese, etc.), and dairy-derived ingredients (e.g., whey protein).

 KETO
Ketogenic eating is very low-carb (50 grams/day; 15 percent or less of a recipe's total calories), low-to-moderate-protein (0.5 to 0.8 grams/pound of lean body mass/day), and high fat: meat, fish, fowl, eggs, nuts and seeds, and high-fat plants like avocado, olives, and coconut. Keto has become extremely popular lately for weight loss, enhanced brain function, improved athletic performance and recovery, and protection against disease, especially cognitive decline.

 **NO ADDED SUGAR**
No sugar or other sweetening agents are used in these recipes. In the recipes that call for sweetening, you will see small amounts of honey, molasses, or maple syrup in their ingredient lists, but they are not "No added sugar" recipes. Natural sweeteners offer a bit more nutritional benefit than processed sugar. It's never advised to use highly processed or chemically altered sweeteners like high-fructose corn syrup.

 VEGAN
Excludes all animal products (e.g., meat, dairy and eggs) and animal-derived ingredients (e.g., honey). Vegans also avoid animal products in not only their food, but their clothing, body care products, and household cleaning agents.

 WHOLE 30
The Whole30 program is a 30-day elimination diet championed by one of our contributors, Melissa Hartwig. It restricts grains, legumes, dairy, sugar, alcohol, carrageenan, MSG, and sulfites. After 30 days, food groups are slowly reintroduced, one at a time, to test your personal sensitivity to each food. Whole30 designates approved products in many categories, from pickles to almond milk to sausage.

For example, Primal Kitchen brand Chipotle Lime Mayo is Whole30 approved, but the homemade preparation for Chipotle Lime Mayo is not, because the adobo sauce you use to make it most likely contains sugar. In contrast, we source a special sugar-free adobo for our manufacturing runs, so the jar in your nearest Whole Foods Market is cool by Whole30. **Whole30.com**, or Melissa Hartwig's book, *The Whole30*, provides extensive details on product options that meet these lofty standards.

Ingredient Substitution Options

In many recipes you will find the icon(s) with the italicized "*option*" next to it. This indicates there are options (located at the bottom of the instructions) to substitute or omit certain ingredients in order to align the recipe with AIP, Dairy Free, Keto, Vegan, or Whole30 guidelines. For example, all the smoothie recipes display the VEGAN *option* and DAIRY FREE *option* icons. Consequently, at the bottom of the page, you see the suggestion to use a vegan or dairy-free protein powder instead of the prescribed Primal Fuel (which contains whey protein, a dairy-sourced agent).

Macronutrient Profiles

Every recipe in this cookbook comes with a macronutrient profile that includes calories per serving, and grams of fat, protein, and carbohydrates. Keep in mind that these numbers can vary significantly depending upon how closely recipes are followed, or if any substitutions or alterations are made to the recipes. If you are going for keto or other precise macronutrient eating patterns, I suggest taking a couple days now and then to measure and journal everything you eat, and enter the results in an online macronutrient calculator, as found at **FitDay.com**, **MyFitnessPal.com**, **SparkPeople.com**, or **PaleoTrack.com**. By the way, recipe macronutrient calculations will even vary depending on what Internet tool you use, so don't stress about it too much. Enjoy your meals, enjoy your life!

Using Primal Kitchen Products in the Recipes

Many of the recipes call for Primal Kitchen brand products, or the homemade version presented in the first recipe section—your choice. The product (or recipe) name is capitalized in the ingredient list (e.g., Avocado Oil, Classic Mayo, or Vanilla Coconut Primal Fuel) for easy identification. If you're going homemade, the page number for the recipe is provided for easy reference. So when it's time to make, for example, Paleo Mayo Waffles (page 67)—I know it sounds crazy but they're incredible—you'll see "½ cup Classic Mayo (page 13)" called out in the ingredients list— indicating to either use the commercial product or make your own by following the Homemade Classic Mayo recipe on page 13 before proceeding with the waffle recipe.

Choosing the Best Foods in Each Category

In a perfect world, all of our meat would be grass fed, our poultry and eggs pasture raised, our fish wild caught, and our fruits and vegetables locally grown and organic. But it's not a perfect world, and the best options are sometimes outside of our budget or difficult to find. In any case, the quality of the food you choose to cook is up to you, and while we didn't list grass-fed, pasture-raised, wild-caught, or organic in the ingredient lists within this book, I highly recommend you do so whenever you can. The same goes for other ingredients such as salt. While you may see it listed simply as "salt" in the ingredients list, I highly recommend using Himalayan pink salt or sea salt. If you would like further discussion and guidance on choosing the healthiest (and avoiding the most objectionable) foods in each category, check out my book, *The New Primal Blueprint*, which has detailed best-to-worst rankings for the Primal Blueprint Food Pyramid categories of meat, fish, fowl, eggs, vegetables, fruits, nuts and seeds, high-fat dairy, dark chocolate, and more.

Without further ado, let's get on with the recipes!

SAUCES
and DRESSINGS

If you know how to grill steak, sauté vegetables, and toss raw greens, then you know how to cook a basic meal. The problem is that basic can get boring really fast. That's why I'm so passionate about healthful, superfood-rich, antioxidant-packed sauces and dressings. The days of "easy on the salad dressing" are over! So pour it on generously and make every bite a nutrient-dense taste sensation.

HOMEMADE
CLASSIC MAYO

SERVES: 8 | **PREP TIME:** 10 minutes

 DAIRY FREE   KETO   WHOLE 30   NO ADDED SUGAR

Homemade mayo only takes a few minutes to make, so you can whip this up right before serving it. However, if you want a slightly thicker texture that's more like bottled mayo, refrigerate it for an hour or more before serving. As a plus, use neutral-flavored avocado oil to eliminate the bitter and sometimes overpowering flavor that extra virgin olive oil can lend to homemade mayo.

1 egg yolk

1 teaspoon (5 ml) lemon juice

¼ teaspoon (1.25 ml) Dijon Mustard (page 39)

1 teaspoon (5 ml) cold water

¼ teaspoon (1.25 ml) salt

¾ cup (175 ml) Avocado Oil

WHISK together the egg yolk, lemon juice, mustard, water, and salt until frothy.

WHISKING constantly, pour the avocado oil in very slowly, only a drop at a time, until the mayo begins to thicken. Once this happens, you can add the oil in a thin stream, whisking until completely combined.

HOMEMADE mayo can stay fresh up to a week in the refrigerator, but usually tastes best if eaten within a few days.

MACRONUTRIENTS: 2 TBSP (30 ML) PER SERVING | CALORIES: 188 | FAT: 21 G | CARB: 0 G | PROTEIN: 0 G

HOMEMADE CHIPOTLE LIME MAYO

SERVES: 4 | **PREP TIME:** 10 minutes

 DAIRY FREE ☀ KETO ♥ NO ADDED SUGAR

Craving mayo with a kick? Our Chipotle Lime Mayo is a spicier version of its classic counterpart. It's perfect for flavoring up your crab cakes, homestyle fries, tuna salads, BLT sliders, fish tacos, and spicy chicken wings. It tastes so good you can even enjoy it as a dip!

1 teaspoon (5 ml) lime juice

1 teaspoon (5 ml) chives, chopped

1 teaspoon (5 ml) garlic powder

1 tablespoon (15 ml) adobo sauce

½ cup (125 ml) Classic Mayo (page 13)

MIX lime juice, chives, garlic powder, and adobo sauce into mayo until thoroughly combined.

HOMEMADE mayo can stay fresh up to a week in the refrigerator, but usually tastes best if eaten within a few days.

MACRONUTRIENTS: 2 TBSP (30 ML) PER SERVING | CALORIES: 209 | FAT: 22 G | CARB: 3 G | PROTEIN: 1 G

HOMEMADE
GREEK VINAIGRETTE

SERVES: 8 | **PREP TIME:** 5 minutes

 VEGAN  DAIRY FREE KETO WHOLE 30 NO ADDED SUGAR

With fresh herb flavor balanced with a hint of sweetness, savory spices, and the zest of fresh lemon juice, this flawlessly balanced vinaigrette is a tantalizing and refreshing complement to any salad. The quintessential addition to roasted chicken or the perfect pairing for heavier fish like mackerel or sablefish—it's a must-have vinaigrette for creative chefs!

½ cup (125 ml) Avocado Oil

⅓ cup (75 ml) red wine vinegar

2 tablespoons (30 ml) apple cider vinegar

1 teaspoon (5 ml) oregano

½ teaspoon (2.5 ml) coriander

½ teaspoon (2.5 ml) marjoram

½ teaspoon (2.5 ml) lemon juice

¼ teaspoon (1.25 ml) oil of oregano

½ teaspoon (2.5 ml) salt

¼ teaspoon (1.25 ml) black pepper

ADD all ingredients to a jar or bottle with a tight-fitting lid and shake until well combined, or blend in a blender to emulsify.

TASTE and adjust seasoning if needed.

MACRONUTRIENTS: 2 TBSP (30 ML) PER SERVING | CALORIES: 123 | FAT: 14 G | CARB: 0 G | PROTEIN: 0 G

HOMEMADE
HONEY MUSTARD VINAIGRETTE

 DAIRY FREE

This succulent dressing packs in the pungency of Dijon Mustard and the sweetness of honey, perfectly enhanced by a tangy, bold touch of lemon. It pairs well with slightly bitter greens like chicory, Belgian endive, escarole, or radicchio, and is tasty enough to be used as a dipping sauce for veggies or to flavor your favorite fish, chicken, or beef dishes. Honey Mustard-braised short ribs, anyone?

½ cup (125 ml) Avocado Oil

2 tablespoons (30 ml) apple cider vinegar

2 tablespoons (30 ml) Dijon Mustard
  (page 39)

1 tablespoon (15 ml) honey

½ teaspoon (2.5 ml) lemon juice

¼ teaspoon (1.25 ml) salt

Water as needed

ADD all ingredients to a jar or bottle with a tight-fitting lid and shake until well combined, or blend in a blender to emulsify.

TASTE and adjust seasonings if needed; add water if consistency needs thinning.

MACRONUTRIENTS: 2 TBSP (30 ML) PER SERVING | CALORIES: 176 | FAT: 18 G | CARB: 3 G | PROTEIN: 0 G

WILD RANCH DRESSING

SERVES: 8 | **PREP TIME:** 10 minutes

 DAIRY FREE   KETO   WHOLE 30   NO ADDED SUGAR

What makes this dressing so perfect is its simplicity. It strikes all the right creamy, tangy, and herbaceous notes using just a few ingredients. Start here, and then personalize the dressing by experimenting with additions like fresh garlic, a drizzle of vinegar, or a spoonful of tamari.

½ cup (125 ml) Classic Mayo (page 13)

½ cup (125 ml) coconut milk

¾ teaspoon (3.75 ml) dill

1 teaspoon (5 ml) chives

¼ teaspoon (1.25 ml) granulated onion powder

⅛ teaspoon (0.625 ml) black pepper

Pinch of salt

IN a large bowl, mix together all ingredients by hand until smooth.

ADD more salt to taste if needed.

MACRONUTRIENTS: 2 TBSP (30 ML) PER SERVING | CALORIES: 124 | FAT: 14 G | CARB: 1 G | PROTEIN: 0 G

ITALIAN VINAIGRETTE

SERVES: 6 | **PREP TIME:** 5 minutes

 VEGAN DAIRY FREE KETO WHOLE 30 NO ADDED SUGAR

This Italian Vinaigrette is a breeze to prepare and will seriously make you crave salads! Made with avocado oil, vinegar, herbs, and spices, this vinaigrette is fresher than any store-bought brand. Consider using fresh herbs if you plan on using it all at once, or dried herbs if you plan to keep it a few days.

¾ cup (175 ml) Avocado Oil

½ teaspoon (2.5 ml) Dijon Mustard (page 39)

3 tablespoons (45 ml) red wine vinegar

1 tablespoon (15 ml) parsley

1 teaspoon (5 ml) oregano

1 garlic clove, minced

¼ teaspoon (1.25 ml) salt

¼ teaspoon (1.25 ml) black pepper

ADD all ingredients to a jar or bottle with a tight-fitting lid and shake until well combined, or blend in a blender to emulsify.

TASTE and adjust seasonings if needed.

MACRONUTRIENTS: 2 TBSP (30 ML) PER SERVING | CALORIES: 244 | FAT: 27 G | CARB: 0.5 G | PROTEIN: 0 G

HOMEMADE CAESAR DRESSING

SERVES: 8 | PREP TIME: 10 minutes

 DAIRY FREE *option*   KETO   WHOLE 30 *option*   NO ADDED SUGAR

Romaine lettuce is at its best topped with Caesar Dressing. Egg yolks are optional; without them the dressing is just as flavorful, but the texture is lighter and more like a vinaigrette. For an even creamier dressing, add finely grated Parmigiano-Reggiano cheese.

2 egg yolks

⅔ cup (150 ml) Avocado Oil

1 tablespoon (15 ml) red wine vinegar

2 tablespoons (30 ml) lemon juice

4 anchovy fillets, mashed into paste

2 garlic cloves, minced

¼ teaspoon (1.25 ml) salt

⅛ teaspoon (0.625 ml) black pepper

½ cup (250 ml) Parmigiano-Reggiano cheese,* finely grated (optional)

WHISK together vinegar, lemon juice, anchovies, garlic, salt, black pepper, and cheese (if using) until well combined in a small bowl.

WHISK in avocado oil and egg yolks.

*OMIT Parmigiano-Reggiano cheese for a dairy-free and Whole30-approved recipe.

MACRONUTRIENTS: 2 TBSP (30 ML) PER SERVING | CALORIES: 180 | FAT: 19 G | CARB: 1 G | PROTEIN: 1 G

HOMEMADE
GREEN GODDESS DRESSING

SERVES: 16 | **PREP TIME:** 10 minutes

 DAIRY FREE KETO WHOLE 30  NO ADDED SUGAR

The most important ingredient in Green Goddess is the herbs, which I generously add to this dairy-free version. Don't worry too much about measuring exact amounts of the herbs—the more the better. Just grab a handful and use cooking shears to snip them into the food processor.

1 cup (250 ml) Classic Mayo (page 13)

¾ cup (175 ml) scallions, chopped

1 cup (250 ml) basil, chopped

¼ cup (60 ml) parsley

1 tablespoon (15 ml) tarragon

¼ cup (60 ml) lemon juice

2 garlic cloves, minced

2 tablespoons (30 ml) anchovies, mashed into paste

2 teaspoons (10 ml) salt

1 teaspoon (5 ml) black pepper

½ avocado

1 tablespoon (15 ml) coconut milk

IN a food processor, combine all ingredients except the coconut milk.

WHILE the food processor is running, add in coconut milk and blend until combined. Transfer to container and store in refrigerator until ready to use.

FOR a thicker dressing or dip, omit the coconut milk.

MACRONUTRIENTS: 2 TBSP (30 ML) PER SERVING | CALORIES: 109 | FAT: 12 G | CARB: 1 G | PROTEIN: 1 G

THOUSAND ISLAND DRESSING

SERVES: 8 | PREP TIME: 5 minutes

 DAIRY FREE

Whether it's used as a salad dressing or as a dip for a burger patty, this dressing adds a rich, zingy flavor, and is a classic many can't do without.

¾ cup (175 ml) Classic Mayo (page 13)

¼ cup (60 ml) Simple Ketchup (page 31)

1 teaspoon (5 ml) white or yellow onion, grated

2 tablespoons (30 ml) dill pickle, finely chopped

2 teaspoons (10 ml) apple cider vinegar

GRATING the onion on the small holes of a box grate rather than dicing it, helps the flavor blend more evenly throughout the dressing.

IN a small bowl, mix the grated onion with the remaining ingredients.

MACRONUTRIENTS: 2 TBSP (30 ML) PER SERVING | CALORIES: 148 | FAT: 16 G | CARB: 2 G | PROTEIN: 1 G

SIMPLE KETCHUP

SERVES: 8 | **PREP TIME:** 10 minutes

 DAIRY FREE

Whip up this flavorful ketchup even when tomatoes aren't in season. Tangy and slightly sweet with just the right blend of seasonings, it's a dead ringer for the bottled stuff.

1 6-ounce (170 g) can tomato paste

¼ cup (60 ml) apple cider vinegar

2 teaspoons (10 ml) honey

1 teaspoon (5 ml) dark or blackstrap molasses

¼ cup (60 ml) water

½ teaspoon (2.5 ml) salt

1 garlic clove, skin removed

1 tablespoon (15 ml) white or yellow onion, grated

Pinch of allspice or garam masala

COMBINE all ingredients in a blender at medium-high speed until very smooth.

CHILL before serving.

MACRONUTRIENTS: 2 TBSP (30 ML) PER SERVING | CALORIES: 27 | FAT: 0 G | CARB: 6 G | PROTEIN: 1 G

BBQ SAUCE

SERVES: 8 | **PREP TIME:** 15 minutes | **COOK TIME:** 35 minutes

 DAIRY FREE

Sweet, tangy, and delicious barbecue sauce without high fructose corn syrup or tons of sugar—just try to find that on the shelves of a grocery store. This primal sauce is sweetened with just a tad of honey and blackberries for a nutritionally dense sauce packed with antioxidants.

2 tablespoons (30 ml) Avocado Oil

1 small red onion, finely chopped

½ cup (75 g) blackberries

2 teaspoons (10 ml) honey

2 tablespoons (30 ml) tomato paste

2 teaspoons (10 ml) apple cider vinegar

1 teaspoon (5 ml) tamari

1 14.5-ounce (411 g) can diced tomatoes in juice

¼ teaspoon (1.25 ml) salt

¼ teaspoon (1.25 ml) paprika

½ teaspoon (2.5 ml) chili powder

¼ teaspoon (1.25 ml) cayenne pepper (optional)

¼ teaspoon (1.25 ml) garam masala

¼ to ½ cup (60 to 125 ml) water

HEAT avocado oil over medium heat in a deep pot. Add onion and sauté for 10 minutes until soft and just barely browned.

IN a food processor, combine onion with the next ten ingredients. Process until smooth.

RETURN to the pot and simmer for 25 minutes over medium to medium-low heat, partially covered so it doesn't splatter too much. Stir frequently to prevent the sauce from sticking to the bottom of the pot.

TURN off heat and stir in garam masala and water. At this point the sauce is not going to taste amazing, but don't panic. The next step is crucial to finishing the sauce.

IN small batches, pour the sauce into a fine-mesh sieve set over a bowl. Push down on the sauce with a spoon so the solids remain in the sieve and the final liquid sauce is extracted into the bowl.

CHILL before serving.

MACRONUTRIENTS: 2 TBSP (30 ML) PER SERVING | CALORIES: 60 | FAT: 4 G | CARB: 6 G | PROTEIN: 1 G

PESTO

SERVES: 8 | **PREP TIME:** 10 minutes

 VEGAN  DAIRY FREE   KETO   WHOLE 30   NO ADDED SUGAR

Creamy, rich pesto is a favorite topping for everything from fish to roasted vegetables. Basil is the most common herb used, but there's no reason you can't make cilantro or parsley pesto. Ditto for the nuts. Try pistachios, walnuts, or even pumpkin seeds. If you miss the richness of cheese in pesto, try blending in a few slices of avocado to smooth out the texture.

½ cup (75 ml) pine nuts

2 to 3 garlic cloves, skin removed

½ to ¾ cup (125 to 175 ml) Avocado Oil

2 to 3 cups (500 to 750 ml) fresh basil leaves

PLACE the nuts and garlic in a food processor and pulse a few times. Add the basil and pulse a few more times.

WHILE the food processor is running, slowly drizzle in the oil. Stop to scrape down the sides as needed.

BLEND until smooth. Salt to taste.

MACRONUTRIENTS: 2 TBSP (30 ML) PER SERVING | CALORIES: 205 | FAT: 22 G | CARB: 2 G | PROTEIN: 1 G

YELLOW MUSTARD

SERVES: 8 | PREP TIME: 5 minutes | COOK TIME: 10 minutes

 VEGAN  DAIRY FREE KETO WHOLE 30  NO ADDED SUGAR

This mustard is made with mustard powder instead of whole seeds. There's a big difference between the two. The main benefit of using powder is that it only takes about 10 minutes to turn it into mustard.

½ cup (125 ml) yellow mustard powder

¾ cup (175 ml) water

¼ cup (60 ml) white wine vinegar

¼ teaspoon (1.25 ml) salt

COMBINE all ingredients in a saucepan over medium heat.

WHISK and stir for 8 to 10 minutes as the mixture comes to a boil and thickens.

CHILL completely before serving.

MACRONUTRIENTS: 1 TBSP (15 ML) PER SERVING | CALORIES: 78 | FAT: 6 G | CARB: 0 G | PROTEIN: 0 G

DIJON MUSTARD

SERVES: 24 | **PREP TIME:** 24 to 48 hours

 VEGAN  DAIRY FREE   KETO   WHOLE 30  NO ADDED SUGAR

Mustard is incredibly easy to make. Soak mustard seeds overnight, then throw them in a blender; that's pretty much it. The results will blow your mind. To make a milder-tasting, less-spicy mustard, use more yellow seeds. For a spicier batch, use more brown seeds.

¼ cup (60 ml) yellow mustard seeds

¼ cup (60 ml) brown mustard seeds

½ cup (125 ml) apple cider vinegar

½ cup (125 ml) water

½ teaspoon (2.5 ml) salt

PUT all ingredients in a non-reactive bowl, cover, and let sit at room temperature for 24 hours.

POUR the entire mixture into a blender. Blend on high until the desired consistency is reached, at least 30 seconds. Keep in mind that the mustard will be grainy and not entirely smooth, since it's made with whole mustard seeds.

IDEALLY, refrigerate the mustard for a day before serving, so the flavor can develop. Mustard tends to taste spicy right after being made, and after a day or two the flavor becomes milder, yet more complex.

MACRONUTRIENTS: 1 TBSP (15 ML) PER SERVING | CALORIES: 23 | FAT: 2 G | CARB: 1 G | PROTEIN: 1 G

TARTAR SAUCE

SERVES: 4 | **PREP TIME:** 10 minutes

 DAIRY FREE   KETO    OPTION    NO ADDED SUGAR

Now that you know how to make Classic Mayo and Dijon Mustard, you can make homemade tartar sauce. Nearly any type of seafood pairs well with this full-flavored sauce.

½ cup (125 ml) Classic Mayo (page 13)

¼ teaspoon (1.25 ml) Dijon Mustard (page 39)

¼ cup (60 ml) dill pickle,* finely chopped

1 tablespoon (15 ml) capers, drained and coarsely chopped

2 teaspoons (10 ml) white onion, grated

1 tablespoon (15 ml) fresh parsley, finely chopped

1 teaspoon (5 ml) lemon juice

TO help the flavor blend more evenly throughout the sauce, grate the onion on the small holes of a box grate rather than dicing it.

MIX the grated onion with the remaining ingredients in a small bowl.

*USE Whole30 Approved dill pickles for a Whole30-approved recipe.

MACRONUTRIENTS: 2 TBSP (30 ML) PER SERVING | CALORIES: 192 | FAT: 21 G | CARB: 1 G | PROTEIN: 1 G

AIOLI

SERVES: 4 | **PREP TIME:** 5 minutes

 DAIRY FREE   KETO   WHOLE 30   NO ADDED SUGAR

Aioli is essentially garlic mayonnaise, but something magical happens when these ingredients are whisked together for a truly dynamic pairing. The bold lemon-garlic flavor and silky texture is a memorable topping for fish and chicken, or as a dip for vegetables. When drizzled lightly over greens, it can be a delicious dressing on its own, too.

½ cup (125 ml) Classic Mayo (page 13)

1 garlic clove, minced

2 to 3 tablespoons (30 to 45 ml) lemon juice

WHISK ingredients together in a small bowl.

MACRONUTRIENTS: 2 TBSP (30 ML) PER SERVING | CALORIES: 191 | FAT: 21 G | CARB: 1 G | PROTEIN: 0 G

BACON DRESSING

SERVES: 4 | **PREP TIME:** 10 minutes | **COOK TIME:** 10 minutes

 DAIRY FREE · KETO · WHOLE 30 · AIP · NO ADDED SUGAR

Warm bacon dressing is especially good over dark greens like spinach and kale. For a breakfast salad, top the greens with a fried egg.

- 4 slices sugar-free bacon
- 1 tablespoon (15 ml) sherry vinegar
- 1 tablespoon (15 ml) parsley, finely chopped
- Avocado Oil as needed

FRY the bacon in a skillet over medium heat. Remove the cooked bacon from the pan and set aside.

POUR the bacon fat into a bowl—you'll need 3 tablespoons of fat. If there isn't enough, add oil.

WHISK together the fat/oil, vinegar, and parsley.

CRUMBLE or chop the bacon into small pieces. Whisk half the bacon crumbles into the dressing. Use the rest as garnish for the salad.

THIS dressing is best when slightly warm, so use immediately or put back in the skillet and heat gently before pouring it over a salad.

MACRONUTRIENTS: 2 TBSP (30 ML) PER SERVING | CALORIES: 158 | FAT: 17 G | CARB: 0 G | PROTEIN: 1 G

ENCHILADA SAUCE

SERVES: 14 | **PREP TIME:** 15 minutes | **COOK TIME:** 30 minutes

 DAIRY FREE   *option*    NO ADDED SUGAR

This enchilada sauce is rich, creamy, and adds the best flavor to homemade enchiladas.

4 tablespoons (60 ml) Avocado Oil

1 tablespoon (15 ml) ghee

1 tablespoon (15 ml) tapioca flour

1 teaspoon (5 ml) garlic powder

1 teaspoon (5 ml) onion powder

½ teaspoon (2.5 ml) cumin

3 tablespoons (45 ml) chili powder

½ teaspoon (2.5 ml) oregano

¾ teaspoon (3.75 ml) salt

¾ cup (175 ml) tomato paste*

4 cups (1000 ml) chicken stock*

ADD oil to a medium-size pot and warm over medium heat.

IN a small bowl, make a paste with the ghee and tapioca flour by smashing with the back of a spoon until creamy.

ADD the ghee/tapioca paste to the pot and stir until well-combined with the oil.

ADD all spices and tomato paste to the pot and stir to combine.

ADD chicken stock, and increase the heat to medium-high. Whisk to remove lumps.

BRING to a boil before reducing the heat to medium. Cook for 30 more minutes, stirring often, until sauce thickens.

*USE Whole30 Approved tomato paste and chicken stock for a Whole30-approved recipe.

SMOOTHIES
and BREAKFASTS

From protein-packed shakes to hearty casseroles, we've got all of your breakfast wishes covered. But don't let the chapter designation "breakfast" restrict how (or when) you cook from this chapter. There's nothing wrong with a couple Primal Scotch Eggs for lunch or a Pepperoni Breakfast Skillet for dinner if that's what you're craving. Better yet, double the recipes so you can eat them for dinner one night and as breakfast the next day.

PEPPERONI BREAKFAST SKILLET

SERVES: 6 | **PREP TIME:** 10 minutes | **COOK TIME:** 12 minutes

 DAIRY FREE · WHOLE 30 *option* · NO ADDED SUGAR

If loving pizza is wrong, I don't want to be right. But pizza isn't always the healthiest option. Here is a healthier take on the classic favorite that will make your taste buds and your body happy!

2 cups (450 g) potatoes, shredded

6 eggs, whisked

2 tablespoons (30 ml) Avocado Oil

8 pepperoni slices*

Seasonings of choice

PREHEAT oven to 375° F (190° C).

ADD avocado oil to a cast iron skillet heated over medium heat.

ADD shredded potatoes and cook for 5 minutes.

ADD whisked eggs and turn off the stove.

ADD pepperoni on top of the eggs and season to your liking.

PLACE the whole skillet in the oven and bake for 10 to 12 minutes.

REMOVE, allow to cool, and serve.

*USE Whole30 Approved pepperoni for a Whole30-approved recipe.

MACRONUTRIENTS: 1 SLICE (⅙ OF SKILLET) PER SERVING | CALORIES: 180 | FAT: 10 G | CARB: 13 G | PROTEIN: 8 G

FENNEL and OLIVE OMELET

SERVES: 2 | PREP TIME: 10 minutes | COOK TIME: 10 minutes

 DAIRY FREE *option*   KETO   WHOLE 30 *option*   NO ADDED SUGAR

If you're tired of throwing the most obvious foods into your morning omelet—mushrooms, spinach, sausage—then this Mediterranean-flavored omelet is just for you. While it's delicious for breakfast, don't hesitate to make this omelet for dinner, too.

4 tablespoons (60 ml) Avocado Oil

1 fennel bulb, thinly sliced
  (fronds removed)

2 to 3 garlic cloves

2 tomatoes, chopped

¼ cup (60 ml) fresh basil, finely chopped

½ cup (125 ml) olives, pitted

Salt to taste

6 eggs, beaten

2 tablespoons (30 ml) Greek Vinaigrette
  (page 17)

Feta or goat cheese* (optional)

WARM 2 tablespoons of avocado oil in a skillet over medium-high heat and add fennel, sautéing until lightly browned. Add garlic and tomatoes and sauté 5 more minutes. Transfer to a bowl and mix in olives and basil. Salt to taste.

WARM remaining avocado oil in a skillet. Add half of the beaten eggs to the skillet. As the eggs cook, use a spatula to lift the edges of the omelet and tilt the skillet so the uncooked egg comes in direct contact with the pan.

AFTER about 3 minutes, when the eggs are mostly set, add half of the tomato mixture and feta or goat cheese (if desired) to one side of the eggs. Using a spatula, fold the uncovered half of the omelet over the top; cook a minute more and slide onto plate.

REPEAT to make second omelet. Top both with Greek Vinaigrette.

*OMIT feta or goat cheese for a dairy-free and Whole30-approved recipe.

MACRONUTRIENTS: 1 OMELET PER SERVING | CALORIES: 668 | FAT: 58 G | CARB: 17 G | PROTEIN: 22 G

Kyle and Devyn Sisson

GROK STAR
SMOOTHIE

SERVES: 1 | **PREP TIME:** 5 minutes

 VEGAN *option*    DAIRY FREE *option*    NO ADDED SUGAR

The subtle vanilla sweetness of this light and fresh smoothie will leave you feeling like a true Grok Star!

1 cup (250 ml) unsweetened coconut milk

1 scoop (20 g) Vanilla Coconut Primal Fuel,* or protein powder of choice

¼ cup (30 g) of ice

1 tablespoon (15 ml) raw almond butter

½ banana

½ cup (125 ml) spinach

¼ avocado

1 tablespoon (15 ml) flax seeds

¼ cup (60 ml) fresh mint

2 dates, pits removed

1 drop vanilla extract

Dash of cinnamon

ADD all ingredients to a blender and blend until smooth.

*USE your favorite vegan or dairy-free protein powder for a vegan-friendly or dairy-free recipe.

MACRONUTRIENTS: 1 ½ CUPS (375 ML) PER SERVING | CALORIES: 566 | FAT: 27 G | CARB: 68 G | PROTEIN: 19 G

Kyle and Devyn Sisson

ALMOND SPICE SMOOTHIE

SERVES: 1 | PREP TIME: 5 minutes

 VEGAN *option*    DAIRY FREE *option*    NO ADDED SUGAR

Thick and creamy, this delectable smoothie delivers a hint of warm spice alongside a dose of healthy fat.

1 cup (250 ml) unsweetened almond milk

1 scoop (20 g) Vanilla Coconut Primal Fuel,* or protein powder of choice

¼ cup (30 g) of ice

½ banana

¼ avocado

¼ tablespoon (4 ml) cacao powder

1 tablespoon (15 ml) coconut oil

1 tablespoon (15 ml) raw almond butter

Dash of cinnamon

Dash of nutmeg

Water as needed

ADD all ingredients to a blender and blend until smooth.

IF smoothie is too thick, add water as needed to thin out.

*USE your favorite vegan or dairy-free protein powder for a vegan-friendly or dairy-free recipe.

MACRONUTRIENTS: 1 ½ CUPS (375 ML) PER SERVING | CALORIES: 476 | FAT: 35 G | CARB: 27 G | PROTEIN: 16 G

N'OATMEAL

SERVES: 2 | **PREP TIME:** 10 minutes

 VEGAN *option*    DAIRY FREE *option*    NO ADDED SUGAR

This hearty and comforting primal breakfast cereal is exactly what you need on mornings when your body is craving a bowl of oatmeal. Coconut flakes, almonds, pecans, and the milk of your choice are blended into a creamy, oatmeal-like cereal that's sweetened with a single Medjool date and topped with fresh berries.

- ¼ cup (60 ml) unsweetened coconut flakes
- ¼ cup (60 ml) raw almonds, preferably soaked overnight, then drained
- ¼ cup (60 ml) raw pecans, preferably soaked overnight, then drained
- ¾ cup (175 ml) unsweetened coconut milk
- 1 tablespoon (15 ml) Vanilla Coconut Primal Fuel,* or protein powder of your choice
- 1 pitted Medjool date, soaked for 10 minutes in hot water
- Pinch of salt

IN a high-powered blender, chop the coconut flakes and nuts until finely ground.

ADD the protein powder, milk, date, and a pinch of salt. Blend until thick and smooth.

WARM the mixture on the stove until hot, or serve cold.

POUR into serving bowls. Add more of your favorite milk, if desired, plus additional add-ins such as fresh berries, butter, or cinnamon.

*USE your favorite vegan or dairy-free protein powder for a vegan-friendly or dairy-free recipe.

MACRONUTRIENTS: 1 ½ CUPS (355 ML) | CALORIES: 585 | FAT: 47 G | CARB: 28 G | PROTEIN: 11 G

CHIPOTLE
BREAKFAST BURRITO

SERVES: 4 to 6 | PREP TIME: 20 minutes | COOK TIME: 20 minutes

 DAIRY FREE *option*  NO ADDED SUGAR

In my mind, a burrito is all about the filling: sensational meat flavored with delicious aromatic spices that send your taste buds on a culinary journey. From there, it's up to you how you want to finish it. I've teamed it here with Chipotle Lime Mayo and avocado salsa, but you could try a tomato salsa, some coleslaw, or fermented chili sauce. Yum! Sure, it's a breakfast burrito, but you should feel free to eat this any time of the day or night.

2 tablespoons (30 ml) Avocado Oil, divided

½ pound (225 g) ground beef

1 teaspoon (5 ml) ground cumin

¼ teaspoon (1.25 ml) ground coriander

½ teaspoon (2.5 ml) chipotle chili powder

½ teaspoon (2.5 ml) onion powder

½ yellow medium bell pepper, diced

2 tomatoes, diced

4 to 6 Cassava Flour Tortillas* (page 135)

1 cup (250 ml) of arugula

4 scrambled or hard-boiled eggs, peeled and quartered

½ cup (125 ml) Chipotle Lime Mayo* (page 15)

1 avocado, diced

1 tablespoon (15 ml) red onion, finely chopped

2 tablespoons (30 ml) cilantro, chopped

2 tablespoons (30 ml) lime juice

Salt and pepper to taste

CHOOSE your preferred style of egg. For scrambled eggs, beat the eggs in a bowl until fully scrambled. Heat avocado oil in a frying pan over medium heat, then pour in the egg mixture. Cook to desired doneness and set aside. For hard-boiled eggs, place eggs in a pot and cover with water. Bring them to a boil, then cover, remove from heat, and let eggs sit for 10 minutes. Once done, place the eggs in a bowl of ice water to cool.

ADD 1 tablespoon (15 ml) of avocado oil to a frying pan over medium-high heat.

ADD the beef, spices, bell pepper, and half of the tomatoes, and cook, stirring occasionally to break up any lumps, for 6 to 8 minutes until the beef is cooked through and the tomato has been broken down.

TO make the Avocado Salsa, combine the avocado, onion, cilantro, lime juice, 1 tablespoon of avocado oil and remaining tomatoes in a bowl and mix gently. Season with salt and pepper and set aside.

FILL the tortillas with a good amount of beef and egg, spoon on some Avocado Salsa and Chipotle Lime Mayo, then top with arugula. Wrap up the tortillas and serve.

*USE Primal Kitchen brand Chipotle Lime Mayo and lettuce wraps/collard greens in place of the Cassava Flour Tortilla, or eat burrito "deconstructed" for a Whole30-approved recipe.

MACRONUTRIENTS: 1 BURRITO PER SERVING | CALORIES: 414 | FAT: 34 G | CARB: 17 G | PROTEIN: 11 G

"We are what we eat, so it makes perfect sense to choose the best quality foods so that our bodies can build the best quality cells. Eating a paleo diet means you'll be consuming foods that are nutrient dense, toxin free, easy to digest, and therefore likely to be the least inflammatory."

—Pete Evans

Kyle and Devyn Sisson

CHIA VANILLA
SWIRL SMOOTHIE

SERVES: 1 | **PREP TIME:** 5 minutes

 VEGAN
option
 DAIRY FREE
option
 NO ADDED
SUGAR

This beauty may look green, but she certainly doesn't taste green!

1 cup (250 ml) unsweetened coconut milk

1 scoop (20 g) Vanilla Coconut Primal
Fuel,* or protein powder of choice

¼ cup (30 g) of ice

¼ avocado

½ cup (125 ml) spinach

2 tablespoon (30 ml) chia seeds

1 drop vanilla extract

2 dates, pits removed

Dash of cinnamon

Water as needed

ADD all ingredients to a blender and blend until smooth.

IF smoothie is too thick, add water as needed to thin out.

*USE your favorite vegan or dairy-free protein powder for a vegan-friendly or dairy-free recipe.

MACRONUTRIENTS: 1 ½ CUPS (375 ML) PER SERVING | CALORIES: 414 | FAT: 19 G | CARB: 52 G | PROTEIN: 14 G

Kyle and Devyn Sisson

MAGENTA
SUNRISE SMOOTHIE

SERVES: 1 | PREP TIME: 5 minutes

 VEGAN *option*    DAIRY FREE *option*    NO ADDED SUGAR

This vibrant smoothie is sweet and tart with a hint of earthy goodness from beets.

1 cup (250 ml) unsweetened coconut milk

1 scoop (20 g) Vanilla Coconut Primal Fuel,* or protein powder of choice

¼ cup (30 g) of ice

¼ cup (40 g) raspberries

¼ cup (40 g) blackberries

¼ cup (60 ml) raw beets, chopped

1 tablespoon (15 ml) chia seeds

1 tablespoon (15 ml) Avocado Oil

1 tablespoon (15 ml) flax seeds

Ginger to taste

ADD all ingredients to a blender and blend until smooth.

*USE your favorite vegan or dairy-free protein powder for a vegan-friendly or dairy-free recipe.

MACRONUTRIENTS: 1 ½ CUPS (375 ML) PER SERVING | CALORIES: 439 | FAT: 31 G | CARB: 26 G | PROTEIN: 16 G

RISE and SHINE
ZOODLE BOWL

SERVES: 2 | **PREP TIME:** 15 minutes | **COOK TIME:** 10 minutes

 DAIRY FREE   *option*   NO ADDED SUGAR

This zucchini noodle breakfast bowl is an easy, healthy breakfast to give you energy to conquer your day!

2 medium zucchinis	2 tablespoons (30 ml) unsweetened almond milk*
2 tablespoons (30 ml) plus 1 tablespoon (15 ml) Avocado Oil, divided	4 slices sugar-free bacon
1 avocado, pitted	2 eggs
1 garlic clove	½ cup (125 ml) tomatoes, chopped
1 tablespoon (15 ml) Chipotle Lime Mayo* (page 15)	Salt and pepper to taste

ADD bacon to a cold skillet. Turn on stove to medium heat. Cook for about 15 minutes, flipping once halfway through. Once cooked, place on a paper towel to drain.

WHILE the bacon is cooking, use a spiralizer to slice the zucchini into noodles.

USING kitchen scissors or a knife, roughly chop the larger zucchini noodles into smaller pieces.

USE residual bacon grease or add 2 tablespoons of avocado oil to the same skillet over medium heat. Add the zucchini noodles and cook for about 5 minutes or until softened.

FOR sauce, use a food processor to blend the avocado, garlic, Chipotle Lime Mayo, almond milk, and 1 tablespoon of avocado oil into a smooth consistency.

ADD the sauce to zucchini noodles. Toss and cook for an additional 2 to 3 minutes.

FRY 2 eggs in a small skillet over medium heat until desired doneness.

POUR the zucchini noodles and sauce into bowls, and top with bacon, fried eggs, and chopped tomatoes. Add salt and pepper to taste.

*USE Primal Kitchen brand Chipotle Lime Mayo and Whole30 Approved almond milk for a Whole30-approved recipe.

MACRONUTRIENTS: 1 BOWL PER SERVING | CALORIES: 425 | FAT: 38 G | CARB: 12 G | PROTEIN: 13 G

PALEO MAYO WAFFLES

SERVES: 5 to 6 | **PREP TIME:** 15 minutes | **COOK TIME:** 10 minutes

 DAIRY FREE

Mixing mayo into your batter might sound a little crazy, but it makes your waffles incredibly moist and fluffy! Don't believe me? Try it once and you'll be hooked!

1 cup (250 ml) coconut flour

1 teaspoon (5 ml) baking soda

1 teaspoon (5 ml) salt

8 eggs

½ cup (125 ml) Classic Mayo (page 13)

½ cup (125 ml) unsweetened coconut milk

¼ cup (60 ml) honey

¼ cup (60 ml) ghee

Avocado Oil for lightly oiling the waffle iron

PREHEAT waffle iron to medium or to your preferred setting. A lower setting makes softer waffles that are lighter in color, while a higher setting makes crispier waffles that are darker in color.

ADD dry ingredients to a medium mixing bowl and combine.

ADD wet ingredients to a large mixing bowl and combine by hand or with a hand mixer.

SLOWLY add dry mixture into wet mixture until well combined. Batter should be light and fluffy.

LIGHTLY oil the waffle iron. Add roughly ¼ cup (60 ml) of batter to the waffle iron, making sure to spread the batter out evenly. Do not overfill.

CLOSE lid and bake for 2 to 3 minutes or until desired level of crispness is achieved.

SERVE immediately or freeze for later use.

MACRONUTRIENTS: 1 WAFFLE PER SERVING | CALORIES: 352 | FAT: 30 G | CARB: 12 G | PROTEIN: 9 G

Kyle and Devyn Sisson

THIN MINT
SMOOTHIE

SERVES: 1 | PREP TIME: 5 minutes

 VEGAN
option  DAIRY FREE
option  NO ADDED
SUGAR

The perfect blend of fresh mint and chocolate, this light and fresh smoothie will satisfy any sweet tooth.

1 cup (250 ml) unsweetened coconut milk

1 scoop (21 g) Chocolate Coconut Primal
  Fuel,* or protein powder of choice

¼ cup (30 g) of ice

¾ teaspoon (3.75 ml) cacao powder

⅓ cup (75 ml) fresh mint leaves

½ cup (125 ml) Swiss chard

¼ avocado

1 tablespoon (15 ml) coconut oil

1 date, pit removed

ADD all ingredients to a blender and blend until smooth.

*USE your favorite vegan or dairy-free protein powder for a vegan-friendly or dairy-free recipe.

MACRONUTRIENTS: 1 ½ CUPS (375 ML) PER SERVING | CALORIES: 402 | FAT: 29 G | CARB: 29 G | PROTEIN: 12 G

Kyle and Devyn Sisson

THE PICNIC BASKET
SMOOTHIE

SERVES: 1 | **PREP TIME:** 5 minutes

 VEGAN *option*    DAIRY FREE *option*   NO ADDED SUGAR

Fruits, veggies, and greens—the smooth and sophisticated flavor of this shake packs all of your favorite picnic treats into one high-protein drink.

1 cup (250 ml) unsweetened coconut milk

1 scoop (21 g) Chocolate Coconut Primal Fuel,* or protein powder of choice

¼ cup (30 g) of ice

¼ cup (60 ml) kale

¼ cup (60 ml) parsley

¼ cup (40 g) blueberries

1 tablespoon (15 ml) Avocado Oil

1 date, pit removed

ADD all ingredients to a blender and blend until smooth.

*USE your favorite vegan or dairy-free protein powder for a vegan-friendly or dairy-free recipe.

MACRONUTRIENTS: 1 ½ CUPS (375 ML) PER SERVING | CALORIES: 392 | FAT: 24 G | CARB: 35 G | PROTEIN: 13 G

MINI BELLS as SHELLS
BREAKFAST TACOS

SERVES: 5 | PREP TIME: 15 minutes | COOK TIME: 15 minutes

 DAIRY FREE   KETO    WHOLE 30 *option*    NO ADDED SUGAR

Mini bell peppers are perfect little edible spoons for these breakfast bites. They're topped with guacamole that's taken up a notch with Chipotle Lime Mayo. I didn't think it was possible to like guacamole more than I already do, but this combo has become a favorite!

10 mini bell peppers

½ cup (125 ml) ground sausage,* cooked and crumbled

2 cups (500 ml) spinach

5 eggs

2 tablespoons (30 ml) ghee

1 avocado, pitted

3 tablespoons (45 ml) Chipotle Lime Mayo* (page 15)

½ teaspoon (2.5 ml) garlic powder

Salt and pepper to taste

PREHEAT oven to 500° F (260° C).

FOR the chipotle lime guacamole, mash one ripe avocado in a bowl with a fork, and then mix in the Chipotle Lime Mayo. Add a tablespoon of water to thin the mixture out if needed, and season with salt and pepper to taste. Store in the refrigerator while you prepare the rest of the dish.

TO transform the mini bells into shells, simply slice off one half of the pepper next to the stem to create a "shell" shape. Be sure to keep the stem intact to make it easy to pick up. Remove the seeds and membrane.

PLACE the mini bell shells cut side down on a foil-lined baking sheet. Roast the peppers until the skin blisters and starts to blacken, then remove from oven and set aside to cool.

WHILE the peppers are roasting, dice the leftover portion of the mini bell peppers and set aside.

IN a large lightly oiled pan, cook the ground sausage until nearly done.

ADD ghee to the pan and let melt. Then add spinach, diced mini bell peppers, and garlic powder, stirring in the sausage. Toss the mixture until the spinach is wilted.

CRACK the eggs into the pan with sausage/spinach mixture. Scramble the eggs by gently stirring them into the mixture.

PLATE the mini bells and spoon your egg mixture into the bells. Top with the guac and eat!

*USE Primal Kitchen brand Chipotle Lime Mayo and Whole30 Approved sausage for a Whole30-approved recipe.

MACRONUTRIENTS: 2 TACOS PER SERVING | CALORIES: 366 | FAT: 28 G | CARB: 15 G | PROTEIN: 13 G

"I used to live by the words 'nothing tastes as good as skinny feels' until I tasted healthy. I have never felt better eating food with a purpose—fueling my body the way it was designed to be fed. It's natural and just makes sense."

—Valerie Grogan, Cocos Paleo Kitchen

OMELET MUFFINS

SERVES: 6 | PREP TIME: 10 minutes | COOK TIME: 20 minutes

 DAIRY FREE KETO WHOLE 30 NO ADDED SUGAR

Keep in mind that while omelet muffins are pretty darn perfect for breakfast on the go, they'd also be great for a weekend brunch. Double the recipe and make a dozen. Then, sit down with family or friends and enjoy the type of long, leisurely breakfast that's so hard to come by during the week.

6 eggs

¼ to ½ cup (60 to 125 ml) cooked meat of your choice, cut or crumbled into small pieces

½ cup (125 ml) diced vegetables of your choice

¼ teaspoon (1.25 ml) salt

⅛ teaspoon (0.625 ml) ground pepper

⅛ cup (30 ml) Classic Mayo (page 13)

⅛ cup (30 ml) water

PREHEAT oven to 350° F (177° C). Generously grease six muffin tins with butter or coconut oil for easier removal, and then line with paper baking cups. The baking cups also help the muffins hold their shape.

IN a bowl, beat the eggs. Add meat, vegetables, salt, ground pepper, and any other ingredients and stir to combine.

SPOON or scoop into the muffin cups.

BAKE for 18 to 20 minutes until a knife inserted into the center of an omelet muffin comes out almost clean. The omelets will continue to cook for a minute or two after removed from the oven. Remove the omelets from the muffin cups and serve, or cool completely and refrigerate for another day.

MACRONUTRIENTS: 1 OMELET MUFFIN PER SERVING | CALORIES: 451 | FAT: 31 G | CARB: 3 G | PROTEIN: 37 G

Kyle and Devyn Sisson

KALE YEAH!
SMOOTHIE

SERVES: 1 | **PREP TIME:** 5 minutes

 VEGAN *option*    DAIRY FREE *option*    NO ADDED SUGAR

This crisp and fresh smoothie will become your newest obsession, morning or afternoon!

1 cup (250 ml) unsweetened almond milk

1 scoop (20 g) Vanilla Coconut Primal Fuel,* or protein powder of choice

¼ cup (30 g) of ice

½ banana

½ cup (125 ml) kale

⅓ cup (75 ml) parsley

½ cup (125 ml) spinach

¼ avocado

2 dates, pits removed

ADD all ingredients to a blender and blend until smooth.

*USE your favorite vegan or dairy-free protein powder for a vegan-friendly or dairy-free recipe.

MACRONUTRIENTS: 1 ½ CUPS (375 ML) PER SERVING | CALORIES: 411 | FAT: 14 G | CARB: 64 G | PROTEIN: 15 G

Kyle and Devyn Sisson

THE HEART BEET SMOOTHIE

SERVES: 1 | **PREP TIME:** 5 minutes

 VEGAN *option*    DAIRY FREE *option*    NO ADDED SUGAR

Beet still my heart! This bright and tart smoothie is sure to make your heart skip a beet!

- 1 cup (250 ml) unsweetened coconut water
- 1 scoop (20 g) Vanilla Coconut Primal Fuel,* or protein powder of choice
- ¼ cup (30 g) of ice

- ¼ avocado
- ¼ cup (40 g) raspberries
- ¼ cup (60 ml) raw beets, chopped
- 1 tablespoon (15 ml) ginger

ADD all ingredients to a blender and blend until smooth.

*USE your favorite vegan or dairy-free protein powder for a vegan-friendly or dairy-free recipe.

MACRONUTRIENTS: 1 ½ CUPS (375 ML) PER SERVING | CALORIES: 237 | FAT: 10 G | CARB: 25 G | PROTEIN: 13 G

PROTEIN PANCAKES

SERVES: 1 | **PREP TIME:** 5 minutes | **COOK TIME:** 10 minutes

 VEGAN *option*　 DAIRY FREE *option*　 NO ADDED SUGAR

Level up your banana-egg pancake recipe by adding 20 additional grams of protein with the help of a high-quality protein powder. Experiment with vanilla or chocolate powders; both work great depending on your taste. Simply follow your kitchen intuition!

2 scoops (40 g) Vanilla Coconut Primal Fuel,* or protein powder of choice

1 banana, mashed

1 egg

Dash of nutmeg and cinnamon

Avocado Oil for cooking

MIX ingredients together, starting with mashed banana, then the protein powder, egg, and spices.

INCORPORATE water, coconut water, or coconut milk to the batter if it's too thick.

NEXT, add avocado oil over medium heat in a griddle pan or skillet. Working in batches, pour or ladle the pancake batter onto the griddle.

LET the pancake cook about 2 minutes per side or until browned.

EAT them plain or add your choice of toppings like grass-fed butter or berries. Serve immediately.

*USE your favorite vegan or dairy-free protein powder for a vegan-friendly or dairy-free recipe.

MACRONUTRIENTS: 6 PANCAKES PER SERVING | CALORIES: 401 | FAT: 16 G | CARB: 38 G | PROTEIN: 28 G

PRIMAL SCOTCH EGGS

SERVES: 4 | **PREP TIME:** 20 minutes | **COOK TIME:** 30 minutes

 DAIRY FREE KETO  WHOLE 30 *option* NO ADDED SUGAR

What could be better for breakfast or an afternoon snack than a Scotch Egg? A Primal Scotch Egg, of course! A Primal Scotch Egg doesn't roll around in flour and breadcrumbs before being fried. The result is an egg that is slightly less crunchy on the outside but no less delicious.

4 eggs

¾ pound (340 g) ground sausage meat*

Avocado Oil for frying

Classic Mayo (page 13) for dipping

HARD-BOIL the eggs by placing them in a pot and covering with water. Bring them to a boil, then cover, remove from heat, and let eggs sit for 10 minutes. Once done, place the eggs in a bowl of ice water to cool.

WHEN cooled, peel the eggs.

DIVIDE the ground sausage meat into four equal portions.

USE your hands to form each portion of the ground meat into a flat pancake a few inches wide. Wrap the meat around an egg, gently shaping it so there are no cracks and the egg is completely hidden.

FOR pan-frying, preheat the oven to 375° F (190° C). Then, pour just enough oil/fat into a deep pan to coat the bottom of the pan. Heat for 2 to 3 minutes over high heat on the stove until the oil is shimmering.

COOK two eggs at a time. Roll the eggs around every few minutes in the oil so all sides of the meat become nicely browned. Cook each egg for about 8 minutes total.

TRANSFER to the oven and cook for 6 to 8 minutes more until the sausage is cooked through.

EAT the eggs warm or cold. Serve alone or with pickles, Classic or Chipotle Lime Mayo, or hot sauce.

*USE Whole30 Approved sausage for a Whole30-approved recipe

MACRONUTRIENTS: 1 PRIMAL SCOTCH EGG PER SERVING | CALORIES: 579 | FAT: 53 G | CARB: 0 G | PROTEIN: 23 G

Kyle and Devyn Sisson

BLUEBERRY DETOX

SERVES: 1 | **PREP TIME:** 5 minutes

 VEGAN *option*    DAIRY FREE *option*    NO ADDED SUGAR

Blueberries and dates blend into a sweet and tart detox drink perfect any time of the day!

1 cup (250 ml) unsweetened coconut milk

1 scoop (20 g) Vanilla Coconut Primal Fuel,* or protein powder of choice

¼ cup (30 g) of ice

½ cup (125 ml) kale

½ cup (80 g) blueberries

¼ avocado

½ banana

2 dates, pits removed

ADD all ingredients to a blender and blend until smooth.

*USE your favorite vegan or dairy-free protein powder for a vegan-friendly or dairy-free recipe.

MACRONUTRIENTS: 1 ½ CUPS (375 ML) PER SERVING | CALORIES: 452 | FAT: 15 G | CARB: 74 G | PROTEIN: 14 G

Laird Hamilton

GROK on a SURFBOARD SMOOTHIE

SERVES: 1 | PREP TIME: 5 minutes

 VEGAN *option*    DAIRY FREE *option*

Blending InstaFuel, Laird's Performance Mushroom Blend, and Primal Fuel not only makes one tasty coffee drink—it makes a healthy one to boot! Add a dash of black pepper to enhance the bioavailability of the fresh turmeric.

- 1 cup (250 ml) unsweetened coconut milk
- 1 scoop (20 g) Vanilla Coconut Primal Fuel,* or protein powder of choice
- ¼ cup (30 g) of ice

- 1 tablespoon (15 ml) InstaFuel
- 2 teaspoons (10 ml) Laird's Performance Mushroom Blend
- 1 teaspoon (5 ml) fresh turmeric

ADD all ingredients to a blender and blend until smooth.

*USE your favorite vegan or dairy-free protein powder for a vegan-friendly or dairy-free recipe.

MACRONUTRIENTS: 1 ½ CUPS (375 ML) PER SERVING | CALORIES: 186 | FAT: 10 G | CARB: 11G | PROTEIN: 10 G

LUNCHES
and SALADS

Don't let the chaos of your work week tempt you into unhealthy lunch choices or bore you to tears with the same bagged salad from the local market. Instead, whip up these delicious meals in minutes, or prep them in advance for a week of satisfying, nutritious lunches on the go.

BLT SALAD BOWL

SERVES: 1 | **PREP TIME:** 15 minutes | **COOK TIME:** 5 minutes

 DAIRY FREE KETO WHOLE 30 NO ADDED SUGAR

Who doesn't love a good BLT every once in a while? This bowl is filled with classic BLT flavors in nourishing salad form. It makes an excellent weekday lunch that is easy to throw together in just a few minutes, or it kicks your dinner up a notch as the side dish for a main course.

1 ½ cups (225 g) greens of your choice

½ avocado

3 slices sugar-free bacon

⅓ cup (75 ml) tomatoes, chopped

2 tablespoons (30 ml) Wild Ranch Dressing (page 21)

COOK the bacon in a skillet over medium-high heat until crispy. Let the bacon cool, and then chop into small pieces.

CHOP the avocado and tomatoes into bite-sized squares.

TOSS the lettuce, avocado, tomatoes, and bacon in a bowl and drizzle with Wild Ranch Dressing.

MACRONUTRIENTS: 1 SALAD PER SERVING | CALORIES: 396 | FAT: 35 G | CARB: 12.5 G | PROTEIN: 12.1 G

ZESTY TUNA WRAPS

SERVES: 4 | PREP TIME: 10 minutes

 DAIRY FREE  NO ADDED SUGAR

I love easy and versatile meals that are perfect for any time of day and easily packable for work or school. The grapes, spinach, walnuts, and lime zest add a crisp, seasonal freshness to the dish, and the Chipotle Lime Mayo wraps it in some delicious mild heat!

2 5-ounce (284 g) cans of tuna

½ cup (125 ml) Chipotle Lime Mayo*
(page 15)

⅓ cup (75 ml) walnuts, chopped

⅓ cup (75 ml) grapes, sliced in half

4 Cassava Flour Tortillas
(page 135)

2 cups (300 g) baby spinach

1 lime for zesting

DRAIN the cans of tuna and flake the meat into a medium bowl.

ADD ¼ cup (60 ml) of Chipotle Lime Mayo, chopped walnuts, and sliced grapes to the bowl of tuna. Mix everything together.

LAY out the tortillas and spread an additional tablespoon of Chipotle Lime Mayo on the center of each wrap.

PLACE ¼ cup (40 g) of baby spinach on each wrap.

ADD tuna salad, and then zest the lime on top. Wrap up your salad and serve immediately.

MACRONUTRIENTS: 1 WRAP PER SERVING | CALORIES: 500 | FAT: 35 G | CARB: 27 G | PROTEIN: 22 G

CHICKEN CAESAR SALAD

SERVES: 4 | **PREP TIME:** 15 minutes | **COOK TIME:** 20 minutes

 DAIRY FREE *option*   KETO *option*    WHOLE 30 *option*    NO ADDED SUGAR

This primal spin on classic Caesar salad adds more nutritional bang for your buck. This makes enough for a group of four, or you can reduce the measurements for a single serving.

2 boneless, skinless chicken breasts

2 teaspoons (10 ml) Avocado Oil

1 large head of romaine lettuce

1 large bunch of red kale

1 cup (250 ml) cherry tomatoes, halved

1 avocado, thinly sliced

4 hard-boiled eggs, halved

⅓ to ½ cup (75 to 125 ml) of Caesar Dressing (page 25)

1 ½ cups (375 ml) of gluten-free croutons* (optional)

Grated Parmesan cheese to taste* (optional)

Lemon wedges for garnish

RUB chicken breasts with 1 teaspoon (5 ml) of avocado oil and season to your liking. Heat the remaining oil in a medium skillet over medium-high heat. Cook for about 10 minutes on each side or until fully cooked. Set aside.

WASH the lettuce and kale, then tear into smaller, bite-sized pieces and add to a big bowl.

SLICE the tomatoes and eggs into halves, and the avocado into thin strips, then add both to the lettuce and kale mixture. Squeeze lemon juice on top.

THINLY slice the chicken and add it, the Parmesan cheese, and gluten-free croutons to the salad.

DRESS the salad with Caesar Dressing before tossing all the ingredients together.

*OMIT gluten-free croutons and Parmesan cheese for a dairy-free and Whole30-approved recipe; omit gluten-free croutons only for a keto-approved meal.

MACRONUTRIENTS: 1 SALAD PER SERVING | CALORIES: 480 | FAT: 36 G | CARB: 25 G | PROTEIN: 18 G

CHIPOTLE LIME EGG SALAD BLT
on SWEET POTATO TOAST

SERVES: 2 to 3 | **PREP TIME:** 10 minutes | **COOK TIME:** 20 to 25 minutes

 DAIRY FREE   WHOLE 30    NO ADDED SUGAR

Sweet potato toast is a great alternative to traditional toast for those of us with celiac disease or gluten intolerance. If you like a bit of spice, and a sweet and savory combination, you will love this recipe!

1 medium to large sweet potato	4 slices sugar-free bacon
2 tablespoons (30 ml) Avocado Oil	1 handful lettuce of your choice
Salt to taste	1 medium tomato, sliced into thick rounds
4 hard-boiled eggs, peeled	Sliced scallions for garnish
2 tablespoons (30 ml) Chipotle Lime Mayo* (page 15)	Sugar-free hot sauce, as topping (optional)

PREHEAT oven to 400° F (205° C) and line a large baking sheet with parchment paper.

WASH and pat the sweet potatoes dry with paper towels. Slice the sweet potato lengthwise to get the longest "toast" possible. (If you are comfortable using a mandolin, hold one end of the sweet potato while you carefully slice the other end to your desired thickness. I like to cut my slices about ¼-inch thick, but you can make them thicker.) Lay the sweet potato slices on the parchment paper.

POUR avocado oil into a bowl and use a pastry brush to lightly coat both sides of the potato slices. Sprinkle the "toasts" with a small pinch of sea salt.

COOK for about 20 minutes, or until the sweet potato toasts are cooked through. They will begin to get crispy on the edges— watch closely after about 18 minutes to make sure they don't burn. Allow the "toasts" to rest on the baking sheet for a few minutes after coming out of the oven to keep them from falling apart. (If your "toasts" are closer to ½-inch slices, they may need up to 22 to 25 minutes to cook all the way through.)

WHILE the sweet potato toasts are cooking, assemble the last ingredients. Cook the bacon in a skillet over medium-high heat until crispy. In a small bowl, chop up the hard-boiled eggs and mix with Chipotle Lime Mayo.

AFTER the toasts have cooled, top with lettuce, bacon (about one slice per "toast"), tomato slices, a scoop of the egg salad, and chopped scallions. Add a dash of hot sauce, if you like a little heat.

*USE Primal Kitchen brand Chipotle Lime Mayo for a Whole30-approved recipe.

MACRONUTRIENTS: 2 SLICES PER SERVING | CALORIES: 407 | FAT: 38 G | CARB: 19 G | PROTEIN: 16 G

"No matter if you have an autoimmune disease, multiple dietary restrictions, or are just trying to eat and feel better, life's too short to eat boring, tasteless food, even if it's healthy."

—Dana Monsees, Real Food with Dana

COCONUT-CRUSTED SHRIMP
FRESH GARDEN SALAD

SERVES: 2 | **PREP TIME:** 20 minutes | **COOK TIME:** 10 minutes

 DAIRY FREE

Whether you are enjoying a beautiful summer evening, or curled up by the fireplace on a cold winter night, this salad always hits the spot with its big, bold flavors and comforting aroma.

½ pound (225 g) wild-caught shrimp (about a dozen, peeled and deveined with tail)

Pinch of Himalayan pink salt

Fresh ground pepper

1 small garlic clove, minced

1 tablespoon (15 ml) Chipotle Lime Mayo (page 15)

1 tablespoon (15 ml) Dijon Mustard (page 39)

⅓ cup (75 ml) unsweetened shredded coconut flakes

1 tablespoon (15 ml) dried parsley

¼ teaspoon (1.25 ml) cayenne pepper

¼ teaspoon (1.25 ml) garlic powder

¼ cup (60 ml) ghee

2 cups (300 g) mixed greens

1 carrot, shaved

½ zucchini, shaved

½ red onion, thinly sliced

1 tablespoon (15 ml) fresh Thai basil leaves

2 to 3 tablespoons (30 to 45 ml) Honey Mustard Vinaigrette (page 19)

1 tablespoon (15 ml) raw pine nuts

IN a small mixing bowl, combine coconut flakes, parsley, cayenne, and garlic powder. Set aside.

IN another bowl, toss shrimp with garlic, salt, pepper, Chipotle Lime Mayo, and Dijon Mustard.

HEAT ghee in a large skillet. Gently toss each shrimp in the coconut flake mixture and coat well. Then, pan fry in one batch for about 3 to 5 minutes on each side or until shrimp are pink and crust is golden brown. Transfer shrimp to a paper towel-lined platter and set aside.

TOSS all salad ingredients together, dress with vinaigrette, and finish with pine nuts.

TRANSFER salad to a serving platter and scatter shrimp on top.

SERVE immediately.

MACRONUTRIENTS: 1 SALAD PER SERVING | CALORIES: 541 | FAT: 43 G | CARB: 17 G | PROTEIN: 26 G

10-MINUTE PAD THAI
ZOODLES

SERVES: 2 | **PREP TIME:** 5 minutes | **COOK TIME:** 5 minutes

VEGAN *option*   DAIRY FREE

Satisfy your takeout craving in less than 10 minutes with this 10-Minute Pad Thai Zoodles recipe using spiralized zucchinis as noodles. The sauce is made with creamy almond butter and coconut aminos, which complement the sautéed zoodles perfectly. You can add an additional egg, or even some chicken or salmon for extra protein.

⅓ cup (75 ml) water

3 tablespoons (45 ml) creamy unsweetened almond butter

1 tablespoon (15 ml) coconut aminos

1 teaspoon (5 ml) chili sauce or hot sauce

2 tablespoons (30 ml) coconut sugar

1 garlic clove, minced

½ lime, juiced

2 tablespoons (30 ml) Avocado Oil

1 egg,* whisked (optional)

½ sweet onion, chopped

3 tablespoons (45 ml) chopped nuts (of your choice)

3 tablespoons (45 ml) scallions, chopped

2 medium zucchinis, spiralized

WHISK together water, almond butter, coconut aminos, hot sauce, coconut sugar, garlic, and lime juice in a bowl and set aside.

IN a medium-sized skillet, heat oil and sauté the chopped onion until translucent.

POUR the whisked egg in with the onion, gently stirring for about a minute to cook the eggs and to break them up into small bits.

STIR in the sauce and spiralized zucchini noodles, or "zoodles," and cook for a couple more minutes.

ADD in the chopped nuts and scallions, cooking for another minute.

DIVIDE into two bowls and serve immediately.

*OMIT egg for a vegan-friendly recipe.

MACRONUTRIENTS: 1 BOWL PER SERVING | CALORIES: 470 | FAT: 39 G | CARB: 29 G | PROTEIN: 12 G

SWEET 'N SPICY SALAD

SERVES: 2 | **PREP TIME:** 5 minutes | **COOK TIME:** 5 minutes

DAIRY FREE
option

This salad is a delightful addition to any meal, but it also shines on its own! It's full of warm apples, spicy arugula, and sweet Honey Mustard dressing—the perfect combination of flavors and textures. The goat cheese is optional, but I think it adds a lovely flavor to the salad.

1 apple, sliced

1 teaspoon (5 ml) coconut oil

2 ½ cups (375 g) baby arugula, packed

1 avocado, sliced

2 tablespoon (30 ml) goat cheese (chévre)*

2 tablespoon (30 ml) toasted pine nuts

2 tablespoon (30 ml) Honey Mustard Vinaigrette (page 19)

PLACE the coconut oil in a small pan and melt over medium heat. Add the apple slices.

COOK the apples for about 5 minutes, flipping the slices occasionally for even cooking, until they become translucent.

WHILE the apples are cooking, place pine nuts in an ungreased skillet on medium-low heat.

COOK the nuts for about 3 to 5 minutes, stirring frequently, until they are golden brown.

DIVIDE the arugula between two bowls. Place the apple slices and avocado on top. Sprinkle the pine nuts and goat cheese on top, and then finish with a drizzle of Honey Mustard Vinaigrette.

*OMIT goat cheese for a dairy-free recipe.

MACRONUTRIENTS: 1 SALAD PER SERVING | CALORIES: 448 | FAT: 39 G | CARB: 24 G | PROTEIN: 9 G

SPINACH and PARMESAN STUFFED CHICKEN BREAST

SERVES: 4 | PREP TIME: 10 minutes | COOK TIME: 1 hour

 KETO    NO ADDED SUGAR

This juicy chicken dish packs a nutritional punch. Batch cook extra breasts for simple gourmet-on-the-go lunches during the week.

- 4 skinless, boneless chicken breasts
- ½ cup (125 ml) Classic Mayo (page 13)
- 1 10-ounce (283 g) package frozen chopped spinach, thawed and drained
- ½ cup (125 ml) shredded Parmesan cheese
- 2 cloves garlic, chopped
- 2 tablespoons (30 ml) Avocado Oil for cooking
- Salt and pepper to taste

PREHEAT oven to 375° F (190° C).

IN a mixing bowl, combine spinach, mayo, Parmesan cheese, and garlic until well blended.

BUTTERFLY the chicken breasts (by slicing or splitting each breast in half without cutting all the way through) to create a pocket in the meat. Spoon the spinach mixture into the pocket of each breast. Place the chicken breasts in a shallow, oiled baking dish and cover.

BAKE for 45 minutes to 1 hour, or until chicken is no longer pink in the center and the juices run clear. An instant-read cooking thermometer inserted into the center of the chicken should read at least 165° F (74° C).

MACRONUTRIENTS: 1 CHICKEN BREAST PER SERVING | CALORIES: 643 | FAT: 26 G | CARB: 6 G | PROTEIN: 92 G

KALE and BLUEBERRY SALAD

SERVES: 1 | **PREP TIME:** 5 minutes

 VEGAN  DAIRY FREE  NO ADDED SUGAR

If you're looking for a quick and easy lunch or antioxidant-rich side salad, then this recipe is ideal. It's very low in sugar and carbs, but has a hint of sweetness from the blueberries. The sliced almonds and onion give it some crunch.

6 ounces (180 g) kale, chopped roughly

10 blueberries

1 tablespoon (15 ml) sliced almonds

¼ red onion, cut into thin slices

1 tablespoon (15 ml) parsley

2 tablespoons (30 ml) Greek Vinaigrette (page 17)

Salt and pepper to taste

TOSS all the ingredients together.

MACRONUTRIENTS: 1 SALAD PER SERVING | CALORIES: 311 | FAT: 21 G | CARB: 27 G | PROTEIN: 11 G

SPICY TUNA
POKE BOWLS

SERVES: 4 | **PREP TIME:** 15 minutes

 DAIRY FREE   WHOLE 30    NO ADDED SUGAR

I didn't realize how amazing poke bowls were until shops starting opening up all over Los Angeles featuring build-your-own poke bowls. After visiting just a few shops, I learned that artificial preservatives and ingredients are often added to poke bowl dishes, so now I create my own bowls using Primal Kitchen Mayo. Poke bowls are great to serve to family and guests, because everyone can tailor their bowl to suit their own taste—so plan your own poke bowl "night in!"

8 cups (1200 g) mixed greens

1 cucumber, thinly sliced

1 cup (250 ml) grated carrots

1 scallion, minced

2 avocados, halved and sliced

1 pound (455 g) wild-caught ahi or yellowfin tuna (sushi grade), diced into ½- to 1-inch cubes

¼ cup (60 ml) Classic Mayo (page 13)

1 tablespoon (15 ml) sesame oil

½ teaspoon (2.5 ml) dried red pepper flakes

1 teaspoon (5 ml) sea salt

1 tablespoon (15 ml) coconut aminos

2 teaspoons (10 ml) black sesame seeds

Finely sliced nori

SET out 4 salad bowls, filling each with 2 cups (300 g) of mixed greens.

DIVIDE the cucumber, carrot, scallion, and avocado between each salad bowl.

IN a separate mixing bowl, add Classic Mayo, sesame oil, dried red pepper flakes, sea salt, and coconut aminos. Whisk to combine.

SLICE the sushi grade tuna (with the grain) into ½- to 1-inch (2.5 cm) bite-sized pieces Add the tuna to the mixing bowl and gently fold until evenly coated with the dressing.

DIVIDE the spicy tuna between the four salad bowls, tossing all the ingredients together.

GARNISH with black sesame seeds and sliced nori (try using kitchen scissors to slice), if you like.

MACRONUTRIENTS: 1 BOWL PER SERVING | CALORIES: 417 | FAT: 23 G | CARB: 21 G | PROTEIN: 34 G

CHIPOTLE LIME
SALMON SALAD

SERVES: 1 to 2 | **PREP TIME:** 10 minutes

 DAIRY FREE    NO ADDED SUGAR

Kick your salmon salad up a notch in both nutrition and flavor by using Chipotle Lime Mayo in place of its classic counterpart, and eat the rainbow with an array of fresh veggies!

1 4-ounce (115 g) can pink salmon

1 celery stalk, chopped

2 tablespoons (30 ml) red bell pepper, chopped

2 tablespoons (30 ml) red onion, chopped

1 to 2 tablespoons (15 to 30 ml) Chipotle Lime Mayo (page 15)

Half a lime, juiced

Salt and pepper to taste

2 cups (300 g) spinach or mixed greens

¼ cup (60 ml) cherry tomatoes, sliced in half

¼ cup (60 ml) cucumber, sliced thinly

¼ cup (60 ml) asparagus, chopped

¼ cup (60 ml) broccoli, chopped

1 hard-boiled egg, chopped

½ avocado, sliced

Lime wedge for garnish

Avocado Oil (optional)

DRAIN the excess liquid from the salmon and flake the fish into a medium bowl.

COMBINE the chopped celery, red bell pepper, onion, lime juice, and mayo with the salmon, adding salt and pepper to taste.

CHOP the ingredients for the salad greens and put into a large bowl.

ADD the salmon salad ingredients on top of the salad greens.

FINISH with freshly squeezed lime juice and a drizzle of avocado oil, if you'd like.

MACRONUTRIENTS: 1 SALAD PER SERVING | CALORIES: 654 | FAT: 43 G | CARB: 32 G | PROTEIN: 39 G

GREEN GODDESS
LETTUCE WRAPS

SERVES: 4 | **PREP TIME:** 5 minutes

 DAIRY FREE   WHOLE 30    NO ADDED SUGAR

These 5-minute lettuce wraps are an easy and nutritious lunch or light snack. The wraps are filled with kelp noodles and nutritious veggies that pair amazingly well with the included Avocado Dipping Sauce recipe. Add chicken or tuna for additional protein, if you'd like.

8 Boston lettuce shells

1 cup (250 ml) kelp noodles

1 avocado, sliced

1 cucumber, sliced

1 green pepper, sliced

1 cup (150 g) fresh spinach

¼ cup (60 ml) scallions, chopped

1 very ripe avocado, for sauce

1 tablespoon (15 ml) Avocado Oil

½ cup (125 ml) Classic Mayo (page 13)

4 tablespoons (60 ml) cilantro

IN a food processor, combine the very ripe avocado, oil, mayo, and cilantro, pulsing until creamy. Pour the Avocado Dipping Sauce into a bowl and set aside.

FOR the lettuce wraps, lay out eight of the lettuce shells on a cutting board.

PLACE kelp noodles, avocado slices, cucumber, green pepper, greens, and scallions in the middle of each lettuce shell. Wrap the ingredients in the lettuce and enjoy with the Avocado Dipping Sauce.

MACRONUTRIENTS: 2 WRAPS PER SERVING | CALORIES: 407 | FAT: 29 G | CARB: 34 G | PROTEIN: 8 G

GRILLED PEACH
and WALNUT SALAD

SERVES: 1 to 2 | PREP TIME: 10 minutes | COOK TIME: 10 minutes

 DAIRY FREE

Peaches, fresh basil, prosciutto, and walnuts make this summer salad a dish you'll crave any time of year! When it comes to dressing, the only suitable option is sweet and tangy Honey Mustard Vinaigrette.

1 large peach, quartered

¼ cup (60 ml) chopped walnuts, raw or toasted

2 cups (300 g) spring greens or fresh spinach

12 leaves fresh basil, whole

2 tablespoons (30 ml) Avocado Oil (for grilling)

4 strips prosciutto, cut in half

3 to 4 tablespoons (45 to 60 ml) Honey Mustard Vinaigrette (page 19)

IF toasting the walnuts, preheat oven to 350° F (175° C).

PREHEAT grill to medium high, or set your broiler to high.

SPREAD walnuts into a single layer on a baking sheet and bake for up to 10 minutes, mixing occasionally to ensure even toasting.

WHILE the walnuts are toasting, quarter the peach and brush the flesh of the peaches with avocado oil to prevent sticking.

GRILL the peaches for about 1 minute on each side of the flesh (no need to grill the skin side), or until deep grill marks form.

TO assemble the salad, toss the greens with the fresh basil leaves. Arrange the grilled peaches and prosciutto slices among the greens, then top with walnuts and a healthy drizzle of Honey Mustard Vinaigrette.

MACRONUTRIENTS: 1 SALAD PER SERVING | CALORIES: 774 | FAT: 65 G | CARB: 32 G | PROTEIN: 26 G

Kendra Cardoza, The Paleo Paparazzi

PROSCIUTTO MANGO
COLLARD WRAPS

SERVES: 4 | **PREP TIME:** 10 minutes | **COOK TIME:** 1 minute

 DAIRY FREE KETO *option*  WHOLE 30 *option*  NO ADDED SUGAR

Few things are as glorious as prosciutto-wrapped mango. That's why I decided not to try and reinvent the wheel—instead I added to it! This wrap includes veggies and a little spice to make for a mouthwatering lunch.

4 large collard green leaves, steamed

1 large mango,* chopped

3 to 4 ounces (90 to 120 g) sliced prosciutto

1 large avocado, chopped

1 large red bell pepper, chopped

Chipotle Lime Mayo* (page 15)

WASH the collard green leaves and pat dry. Place leaves on a cutting board and with a knife, cut each side of the stem, leaving about 2 inches of the top still attached. Cut off the top portion of the stem to remove. (You'll see why we didn't remove all the way in step 3.)

ADD the leaves to a steamer and steam for 30 seconds to 1 minute, just long enough to wilt.

REMOVE the leaves from the steamer and place on the cutting board. Take a leaf and cut all the way through to the top of the stem to form two separate halves. Take the two halves and overlap them one on top of the other (cut sides together). Repeat with the other 3 leaves.

SLATHER a generous amount of Chipotle Lime Mayo on each of the 4 leaf pairs, add a few slices of prosciutto and a handful of chopped mango, avocado, and bell pepper to the center. Take the sides of the leaves and fold them over; then take the bottom part and fold it on top, tucking and rolling as you would if you were wrapping a burrito.

EAT as is or slice down the middle. Add toothpicks to hold in place if needed when serving. Dip the wrap in some more Chipotle Lime Mayo, if you'd like.

*USE Primal Kitchen brand Chipotle Lime Mayo for a Whole30-approved recipe. Omit mango for a keto-approved recipe.

MACRONUTRIENTS: 1 WRAP PER SERVING | CALORIES: 210 | FAT: 13 G | CARB: 16 G | PROTEIN: 10 G

BANH MI SALAD

SERVES: 4 | PREP TIME: 20 minutes | COOK TIME: 10 minutes

 DAIRY FREE KETO  *option*  NO ADDED SUGAR

Banh Mi is a popular Vietnamese sandwich with a sweet, savory, tangy, and sometimes spicy blend of meat, raw vegetables, and herbs. Freed from the confines of a baguette, the bold flavors and contrasting textures of Banh Mi also make an incredible salad.

1 pound (455 g) of pork loin, sliced into ½-inch (1 cm) pieces

3 garlic cloves, thinly sliced or pressed

2 tablespoons (30 ml) fish sauce*

1 teaspoon (5 ml) black pepper

5 cups (½ large head) cabbage, grated

1 cup (250 ml) carrot, grated

1 to 2 cups (250 to 500 ml) cucumber, thinly sliced or chopped

2 green onions, chopped

Handful of mint and cilantro leaves, torn into pieces

1 jalapeño and 1 radish, thinly sliced (optional)

¼ cup (60 ml) Classic Mayo (page 13)

2 tablespoons (30 ml) unseasoned rice vinegar (or fresh lime juice)

COMBINE pork, garlic, fish sauce, and black pepper in a sealed bag or container. Marinate the ingredients while you prepare the rest of the dish.

IN a small bowl, whisk together Classic Mayo and rice vinegar. (If you like a lot of dressing on your salad, double the measurements.) Set aside.

COMBINE all vegetables and herbs in a large bowl.

HEAT several tablespoons of avocado oil in a large cast iron skillet over medium-high heat. Add the pork and sear for 3 to 4 minutes on each side. Once the pork is cooked through, remove it from the pan and slice the pork medallions into thin strips. Add pork strips to the salad, and mix.

Pour the dressing on top. Toss well and serve.

*USE Whole30 Approved fish sauce for a Whole30-approved recipe.

MACRONUTRIENTS: 1 SALAD PER SERVING | CALORIES: 345 | FAT: 20 G | CARB: 13 G | PROTEIN: 27 G

SALMON CAKES

SERVES: 2 to 3 | **PREP TIME:** 10 minutes | **COOK TIME:** 15 minutes

 DAIRY FREE · KETO · WHOLE 30 · NO ADDED SUGAR

Like crab cakes? Then you're going to love these quick and easy salmon cakes. They're satisfying and good for you. Serve with a green salad for a complete meal, or as an appetizer.

1 4-ounce (115 g) can of pink salmon

¼ cup (60 ml) Classic Mayo (page 13)

1 teaspoon (5 ml) Dijon Mustard (page 39)

1 egg, lightly beaten

½ cup (125 ml) flax meal (split into two ¼ cup (60 ml) portions)

Kosher salt and freshly ground black pepper

2 tablespoons (30 ml) fresh flat leaf parsley, chopped

2 tablespoons (30 ml) fresh dill, chopped

2 tablespoons (30 ml) fresh chives, chopped

2 to 3 tablespoons (30 to 45 ml) Tartar Sauce (page 41)

DRAIN the excess liquid from the salmon and flake the fish into a large bowl. Add the mayo, mustard, and egg.

IN a small bowl, mix all fresh herbs together.

ADD 4 tablespoons (60 ml) of fresh herbs and ¼ cup (60 ml) of flax meal to the salmon mixture. Mix to incorporate.

SHAPE into four to six cakes. Dust outside cakes with a little more flax meal.

HEAT 4 tablespoons (60 ml) of avocado oil in a large sauté pan over medium heat. In batches, add the salmon cakes and fry for 3 to 4 minutes on each side, until browned. Drain on paper towels; keep warm in a preheated 250° F (130° C) oven.

SERVE cakes with Tartar Sauce and sprinkle with remaining fresh herbs.

MACRONUTRIENTS: 2 SALMON CAKES PER SERVING | CALORIES: 514 | FAT: 48 G | CARB: 10 G | PROTEIN: 19 G

OYSTER PO' BOY SALAD

SERVES: 2 | **PREP TIME:** 15 minutes | **COOK TIME:** 10 minutes

 DAIRY FREE WHOLE 30  NO ADDED SUGAR

An oyster po' boy is a classic New Orleans sandwich made of oysters breaded in cornmeal and fried until crisp. Set on a white roll and slathered in mayo, the oysters are topped with iceberg lettuce and tomatoes. It isn't exactly health food. But if you ditch the white bread and cornmeal, and perhaps substitute in some romaine lettuce for the iceberg, the oyster po' boy can be reincarnated as a salad that's delicious in its own right.

½ head romaine lettuce, thinly sliced

2 tomatoes, sliced

1 cup (250 ml) Classic Mayo (page 13)

1 teaspoon (5 ml) Dijon Mustard (page 39)

1 tablespoon (15 ml) lemon juice

½ teaspoon (2.5 ml) smoked paprika (or to taste)

1 tablespoon (15 ml) capers, drained

1 tablespoon (15 ml) parsley, finely chopped

12 to 16 shucked fresh oysters

¾ cup (175 ml) tapioca flour

½ teaspoon (2.5 ml) kosher salt

½ teaspoon (2.5 ml) cayenne pepper

2 egg whites

Avocado Oil for frying

IN a large bowl, combine the lettuce and tomatoes. Set aside.

IN a small bowl, whisk together mayo, mustard, lemon juice, smoked paprika, capers, and parsley. Refrigerate until ready to toss the salad.

IN a medium bowl or on a rimmed plate, mix together the tapioca flour, salt, and cayenne pepper. Set aside.

IN a large bowl, whisk the egg whites until frothy. Add oysters to the egg whites, stirring so the oysters are well coated. Remove the oysters with a fork or slotted spoon, leaving behind any of the egg white liquid that isn't clinging to the oysters.

ONE by one, dredge the oysters through the tapioca flour, coating each side.

POUR the avocado oil into a deep, heavy pot (using ¼- to ½-inch [6 to 13 mm] of oil for frying). Heat the oil on medium-high until it is shimmering. Test the oil temperature by tossing in a tiny fleck of the tapioca flour; it should bubble and fry immediately.

COOK the oysters in two batches for 2 minutes on each side, until lightly browned and crispy. Add to the bowl of lettuce and tomatoes. Toss with the salad dressing.

MACRONUTRIENTS: 1 SALAD PER SERVING | CALORIES: 989 | FAT: 91 G | CARB: 19 G | PROTEIN: 26 G

"I don't eat a single bite of food that I don't absolutely love."

—Mark Sisson

PORK LOIN SALAD
with DATE VINAIGRETTE

SERVES: 2 | PREP TIME: 15 minutes | COOK TIME: 10 minutes

 DAIRY FREE WHOLE 30 AIP  NO ADDED SUGAR

In this recipe, a surprising combination of ingredients come together in an unforgettable way, resulting in a sweet, salty, and garlicky salad that's downright addictive.

½ pound (225 g) pork loin	½ cup (125 ml) Avocado Oil
4 dates, pitted	1 tablespoon (15 ml) sherry vinegar
6 anchovy fillets	1 fennel bulb
Zest of 1 large lemon, grated	4 handfuls of mixed salad greens
2 garlic cloves	

SLICE the pork loin into rounds no more than 1-inch thick. Lightly salt and pepper the meat and set aside.

IN a food processor or blender, process the dates, anchovies, lemon zest, garlic cloves, avocado oil, and sherry vinegar until the vinaigrette has a thick, chunky texture.

REMOVE the stem and fronds from the fennel and cut the bulb in half, discarding the inner core. Slice each half into very thin strips. If you have a mandoline, use it to slice the fennel paper-thin.

HEAT a few tablespoons of avocado oil in a skillet over medium heat. Add the fennel, sautéing until lightly browned—about 3 minutes for slightly crunchy fennel, longer to soften the texture and make the flavor milder.

ADD the pork to the skillet and as the first side cooks, spread about a teaspoon of the vinaigrette onto each piece. After 3 minutes, flip the pork medallions and cook just a few minutes more, so the outside of the meat is browned but the inside is still a bit pink.

TOSS the salad greens with the remaining vinaigrette and divide onto two plates. Top with the fennel and pork.

MACRONUTRIENTS: 1 SALAD PER SERVING | CALORIES: 912 | FAT: 69 G | CARB: 49 G | PROTEIN: 31 G

STARTERS
and SMALL BITES

Every party needs hors d'oeuvres, and leftover appetizers make the perfect midday snack for the next day. Whether you're looking for hand-held nibbles or delicious dips, we've got you covered with tasty and healthful starters sure to be the life of any party, especially of the primal kind!

TRI-OLIVE DIP

SERVES: 6 to 8 | **PREP TIME:** 5 minutes

 VEGAN   DAIRY FREE   KETO   WHOLE 30 AIP *option*   NO ADDED SUGAR

Dips and sauces can literally transform a regular meal into something extra special and worth repeating. This tri-olive dip is simple to prepare and bursting with flavor, in part due to Primal Kitchen's Extra Virgin Avocado Oil, which is everything an oil should be—delicate, but strong; light, but with depth in every bite. You can add this dip to a salad bowl for extra zing and healthy fat, use it to marinate meats, toss it with sautéed veggies, or sprinkle it on as a garnish for your next breakfast scramble. Try making it today and see how you prefer it best. The possibilities are endless!

- 1 cup (250ml) canned green olives (sulfite free)
- 1 cup (250 ml) canned black olives (sulfite free)
- ½ cup (125 ml) Kalamata olives, pits removed (sulfite free)
- ½ cup (125 ml) Primal Kitchen Extra Virgin Avocado Oil

- 1 cup (250 ml) fresh parsley
- 1 cup (250 ml) fresh cilantro
- 1 small garlic clove
- ½ teaspoon (2.5 ml) dried red pepper flakes*
- 2 tablespoon (30 ml) fresh lime juice
- ¼ teaspoon (1.25 ml) sea salt

PLACE all ingredients except avocado oil into a food processor and pulse on high speed just until olives are broken up, about 5 seconds.

SLOWLY add avocado oil with the motor running, turning off to scrape the sides of the food processor bowl. Continue pulsing until all ingredients resemble a tapenade (roughly minced texture, but not a puree).

STORE in the refrigerator for up to one week. Add to salads, veggies, and meats, or use as a dip for carrot, celery, or jicama sticks.

*OMIT dried red pepper flakes for an AIP-friendly recipe.

MACRONUTRIENTS: 2 TBSP (30 ML) PER SERVING | CALORIES: 239 | FAT: 25 G | CARB: 4.5 G | PROTEIN: 1 G

TUNA-STUFFED
GRILLED JALAPEÑO POPPERS

SERVES: 5 | **PREP TIME:** 10 minutes | **COOK TIME:** 8 minutes

 DAIRY FREE   KETO   WHOLE 30   NO ADDED SUGAR

A fresh jalapeño pepper is the perfect delivery vehicle for a nibble of tuna salad. A stuffed jalapeño can be eaten with your fingers in one or two bites, and the addictive spicy flavor keeps you coming back for more.

1 5-ounce can (142 g) tuna fish, packed in water

¼ red bell pepper, finely chopped

4 green onions, finely chopped

Handful of cilantro, finely chopped

½ avocado

3 tablespoons (45 ml) Classic Mayo (page 13)

1 teaspoon (5 ml) garlic powder

Salt and pepper to taste

5 large jalapeño peppers

COMBINE tuna, red pepper, green onions, cilantro, avocado, and mayo in a bowl.

SEASON tuna mixture with garlic powder, salt, and pepper to taste.

TUNA mixture can be stored in the refrigerator for a couple days, or can be used immediately.

CUT jalapeño peppers in half lengthwise and remove seeds.

STUFF the jalapeños with tuna mixture.

GRILL over medium heat for about 8 minutes.

SERVE while still hot from the grill.

MACRONUTRIENTS: 2 POPPERS PER SERVING | CALORIES: 128 | FAT: 10 G | CARB: 4 G | PROTEIN: 7 G

BAKED
BISON MEATBALLS

SERVES: 5 to 6 | **PREP TIME:** 15 minutes | **COOK TIME:** 18 minutes

 DAIRY FREE   KETO   WHOLE 30 *option*   NO ADDED SUGAR

These meatballs combine the flavors of savory bison meat and tangy Chipotle Lime Mayo to create a simple dish that can be prepared ahead of time and frozen, then thawed and baked until fully cooked. They are perfect for parties, evening dinners, or grab-and-go meals during a busy weekend.

1 pound (455 g) ground bison

1 pound (455 g) ground Italian sausage*

3 tablespoon (45 ml) Chipotle Lime Mayo* (page 15)

1 teaspoon (5 ml) Worcestershire sauce*

¼ red onion, diced

½ cup (125 ml) spinach, chopped

Salt and pepper to taste

PREHEAT oven to 400° F (200° C).

IN a bowl, mix all ingredients until well combined.

LINE a baking sheet with parchment paper.

SCOOP about 1 tablespoon of meatball mixture and form into a ball.

CONTINUE until all the meat is formed into meatballs (approximately 20 to 24 meatballs); then line them up, about 1 inch (2.5 cm) apart on the parchment-lined baking sheet.

BAKE for 16 to 18 minutes.

*USE Primal Kitchen brand Chipotle Lime Mayo, Whole30 Approved sausage, and omit Worcestershire sauce for a Whole30-approved recipe.

MACRONUTRIENTS: 4 MEATBALLS PER SERVING | CALORIES: 431 | FAT: 82 G | CARB: 6 G | PROTEIN: 30 G

CASSAVA FLOUR
TORTILLAS

SERVES: 8 | **PREP TIME:** 20 minutes | **COOK TIME:** 15 minutes

 VEGAN  DAIRY FREE AIP  NO ADDED SUGAR

This gluten-free recipe for tortillas will taste better than any tortilla recipe you've tried! Give it a whirl.

1 cup (250 ml) cassava flour

1 teaspoon (5 ml) coarse-ground sea salt

3 tablespoons (45 ml) Avocado Oil

½ to 1 cup (125 to 250 ml) warm water

IN a medium-sized bowl, add cassava flour and sea salt.

MIX the dry ingredients, then add avocado oil and warm water a tablespoon at a time.

KNEAD the mixture with your hands until you can form a big ball. The dough should be moldable and not sticky.

DIVIDE the ball of dough into eight equal portions.

FORM each ball into a tortilla using a tortilla press, rolling pin, or your hands.

TRANSFER the tortilla to a dry cast iron skillet over medium heat, and cook for 2 minutes on each side.

REMOVE from heat and cover with a kitchen towel to keep warm until serving.

MACRONUTRIENTS: 1 TORTILLA PER SERVING | CALORIES: 108 | FAT: 6 G | CARB: 13 G | PROTEIN: 0 G

Marla Sarris & Ana Navarro, Paleo MX

FISH QUESADILLAS

SERVES: 3 to 4 | **PREP TIME:** 20 minutes | **COOK TIME:** 30 minutes

 DAIRY FREE    NO ADDED SUGAR

These authentic Mexican fish quesadillas are a common treat found in Tianguis (Mexican farmers' markets). You can also find them in shacks along the coast of Mexico. Now they can easily be made in your kitchen too!

Cassava Flour Tortillas (page 135)

½ onion, chopped

¾ pound (340 g) tomatoes, chopped

1 jalapeño pepper, chopped

1 pound (455 g) wild-caught tilapia, chopped

1 teaspoon (5 ml) coarse-ground sea salt

2 to 3 tablespoons (30 to 45 ml) lard

Classic Mayo (page 13)

1 avocado, sliced

1 lime

Hot sauce

MAKE Cassava Flour Tortillas and set aside.

ADD onions to a cast iron skillet over medium heat and cook for 5 minutes.

ADD chopped tomatoes and jalapeño pepper and cook until tomatoes release their juices (approximately 5 minutes). Add tilapia and sea salt. Mix well and cook until juices have reduced.

GRAB a tortilla and fill it with the cooked tilapia. Fold the tortilla in half and stack on a plate. Repeat with remaining tortillas.

MELT lard in a cast iron skillet over medium heat. Once sizzling hot, fry quesadillas in batches of two or three until golden and crispy. Don't crowd the pan. Transfer fried quesadillas to a plate covered with a paper towel. Repeat until all quesadillas are fried.

FORM an assembly line of mayo, avocado slices, lime halves, and hot sauce. Open each quesadilla and spread a layer of mayo, followed by a slice or two of avocado, a drizzle of lime juice, and a splash of hot sauce.

SERVE warm.

MACRONUTRIENTS: 2 QUESADILLAS PER SERVING | CALORIES: 529 | FAT: 27 G | CARB: 21 G | PROTEIN: 34 G

HONEY MUSTARD WINGS

SERVES: 5 | PREP TIME: 1 hour 15 minutes | COOK TIME: 40 minutes

 DAIRY FREE KETO

Wings are the perfect food for uniting with friends on the weekend while watching the big game, or gathering your family around the table for a healthier version of an old favorite like I've done with this easy wing recipe for my own loved ones.

2 pounds (900 g) wings, fresh or thawed, if previously frozen

1 cup (250 ml) Honey Mustard Vinaigrette (page 19)

Juice of ½ a lemon

Zest of ½ a lemon

IN a large plastic storage bag, combine wings with all the other ingredients and marinate for at least 30 minutes. (Ideally allow to marinate for an hour or more.)

ONCE they have marinated, preheat grill to approximately 400° F (200° C).

COOK for 40 minutes, turning as needed to avoid burning.

TO really amp up the lemon flavor, spritz with the juice of ½ a lemon after grilling, or brush with more Honey Mustard Vinaigrette.

SERVE immediately.

MACRONUTRIENTS: 4 WINGS PER SERVING | CALORIES: 738 | FAT: 59 G | CARB: 6 G | PROTEIN: 43 G

SPINACH DIP

SERVES: 6 | PREP TIME: 10 minutes

 DAIRY FREE    NO ADDED SUGAR

Skip the heavy, calorie-laden dips and turn to this healthier, paleo version of the party favorite—spinach dip! Perfect with veggies or crackers, this dip is sure to be a hit any time you serve it.

- 1 10-ounce (283 g) package frozen chopped spinach, thawed and drained
- 1 cup (250 ml) coconut cream*
- 1 cup (250 ml) Classic Mayo (page 13)
- ½ tablespoon (7.5 ml) dried parsley
- ¼ tablespoon (3.75 ml) dried dill
- ¼ tablespoon (3.75 ml) dried chives

- 1 teaspoon (5 ml) onion powder
- 1 teaspoon (5 ml) garlic powder
- 1 tablespoon (15 ml) lemon juice
- ½ cup (125 ml) medium red bell pepper, diced
- 1 8-ounce can (226 g) water chestnuts, chopped

IN a small bowl, stir together coconut cream and mayo.

IN a large bowl, combine spinach, mayo mixture, and remaining ingredients. Stir well to combine.

REFRIGERATE for at least 2 hours before serving.

MACRONUTRIENTS: ½ CUP (125 ML) PER SERVING | CALORIES: 491 | FAT: 38 G | CARB: 37 G | PROTEIN: 5 G

NO RICE
SPICY TUNA ROLLS

SERVES: 3 | **PREP TIME:** 20 minutes

 DAIRY FREE   KETO   WHOLE 30 *option*   NO ADDED SUGAR

Who's the real star of a spicy tuna roll? The spicy tuna, of course! These rolls cut out the bulky rice and bring the fiery flavors of spicy tuna front and center. Perfect as a quick bite or appetizer!

½ pound (225 g) sushi grade tuna, diced

1 tablespoon (15 ml) Classic Mayo (page 13)

1 tablespoon (15 ml) sriracha sauce*

¾ cucumber, julienned

1 tablespoon (15 ml) fresh ginger, julienned

1 avocado, sliced

1 tablespoon (15 ml) green onions, finely sliced

3 nori sheets, cut in half

1 tablespoon (15 ml) black sesame seeds for garnish (optional)

Wasabi* (optional)

Coconut aminos (optional)

Ginger, grated (optional)

PREP cucumber, ginger, avocado, and green onions. Set aside.

DICE tuna and place into a medium-sized bowl. Add mayo and sriracha, and stir until all tuna pieces are evenly coated.

CAREFULLY fold a nori sheet back and forth until it breaks and you have two half rectangular pieces.

PLACE the half nori sheet in your left hand and carefully add ⅓ of the avocado on top of the nori at a diagonal. The avocado should hit the bottom left corner of the nori sheet but not the top right, so move it slightly over to the right to make for easy rolling.

ONCE the avocado is placed, add a bit of tuna. Follow with cucumber, ginger, and green onions. Finally, add the black sesame seeds.

ONCE all ingredients are placed onto the nori sheet, gently roll it so that the bottom left corner becomes the opening and the top right becomes the bottom, tucked end of the roll.

TO get the nori sheets to stick, wet edge with moistened fingers and rub.

CONTINUE with the other two rolls until you have six hand rolls.

DIP into coconut aminos and top with a little wasabi and grated ginger if you'd like.

*USE Whole30 Approved wasabi and hot sauce for a Whole30-approved recipe.

MACRONUTRIENTS: 2 ROLLS PER SERVING | CALORIES: 300 | FAT: 19 G | CARB: 11 G | PROTEIN: 22 G

"I would be lying if I said that preparing home-cooked meals didn't require some extra time and effort. However, the privilege of being able to handpick every single ingredient and the joy of eating something you've prepared with your own hands is an experience that I've always found to be well worth it."

—Anya Kaats, Anya's Eats

CHIPOTLE AVOCADO CHORIZO FUN-DIPPO

SERVES: 6 | **PREP TIME:** 20 minutes | **COOK TIME:** 50 minutes

DAIRY FREE *option*   KETO   NO ADDED SUGAR

If you're looking for an ooey gooey party dip that pleases every palate, look no further than this Fun-Dippo! And get creative with your dippers—raw veggies or sweet potato fries work great!

½ cup (125 ml) Chipotle Lime Mayo (page 15)

2 large (or 4 to 6 small) avocados, diced

½ medium tomato, diced

¼ cup (60 ml) cilantro, finely chopped

½ cup (125 ml) green onion, diced

2 to 3 garlic cloves, minced

Salt and pepper to taste

12 ounces (350 g) chorizo

½ onion, chopped

¾ cup (175 ml) jack cheese*

¾ cup (175 ml) Mozzarella (or queso fresco)*

1 jalapeño, finely chopped (optional)

PREHEAT oven to 375º F (190° C).

HEAT a large cast iron skillet over medium-high heat. Crumble and cook chorizo, garlic, and onion. Turn off heat when meat is thoroughly cooked (about 15 minutes) and spread the mixture flat across the pan. Evenly sprinkle ¼ cup (60 ml) of each cheese over the chorizo mixture.

IN a separate bowl, combine the Chipotle Lime Mayo, avocado, tomato, cilantro, green onion, salt, garlic, jalapeño, and ¼ cup (60 ml) of each cheese. No need to mash the mixture; there should be little chunks of avocado.

SPREAD this mixture evenly across the top of the chorizo and cheese and bake for 25 minutes.

REMOVE the skillet from oven. Turn up the heat to 400º F (200° C) and sprinkle the remaining cheese evenly across the top of the dish before cooking for 10 more minutes. Once finished, avocado should look a little crispy with melted crisp cheese on top.

*USE cashew cheese or your favorite cheese alternative for a dairy-free recipe.

MACRONUTRIENTS: ½ CUP (125 ML) PER SERVING | CALORIES: 721 | FAT: 62 G | CARB: 13 G | PROTEIN: 31 G

"CHEESY"
ZUCCHINI SLICES

SERVES: 5 TO 6 | **PREP TIME:** 15 minutes | **COOK TIME:** 23 minutes

 DAIRY FREE · KETO · WHOLE 30 · NO ADDED SUGAR

Got a hankering for pizza, but it doesn't fit into your macros? No sweat! These "cheesy" baked squash slices are sure to curb your craving. If you've never baked mayo before, you're missing out. The egg cooks up and creates a delicious coating over the food, like cheese! Add in some garlic, spices, and green onion, and you're all set!

2 large zucchinis, sliced

1 tablespoon (15 ml) Avocado Oil

1 teaspoon (5 ml) salt

1 teaspoon (5 ml) pepper

4 garlic cloves, minced

1 green onion, finely chopped

4 to 5 tablespoons (60 to 75 ml) Classic Mayo (page 13)

PREHEAT oven to 425° F (220° C). Oil a sheet pan (or two) with avocado oil.

SLICE your zucchinis lengthwise into roughly ½-inch slices, and line them up on the sheet pan (or two).

SPRINKLE the garlic, salt, and pepper all over the zucchini.

SMEAR about ½ tablespoon (8 ml) Classic Mayo generously over each slice. Then sprinkle the green onion over it.

BAKE for 20 minutes. From there, hit them with the broiler for 2 to 3 minutes to achieve a nice brown color.

YOU can also add ground sausage, cherry tomatoes, olives, etc! Go crazy with the possibilities.

MACRONUTRIENTS: 2 SLICES PER SERVING | CALORIES: 99 | FAT: 10 G | CARB: 1 G | PROTEIN: 0.4 G

BACON-WRAPPED SHRIMP
STUFFED PORTABELLAS

SERVES: 6 | PREP TIME: 45 to 60 minutes | COOK TIME: 30 to 70 minutes

 DAIRY FREE   WHOLE 30    NO ADDED SUGAR

Deliciously meaty portabellas are perfect on their own—add bacon-wrapped shrimp into the mix and you've got yourself an epic bite!

12 portabella mushrooms, washed and patted dry

2 white sweet potatoes

12 shrimp, tails on

6 slices of sugar-free bacon, cut in half

3 tablespoons (45 ml) ghee

1 cup (250 ml) Greek Vinaigrette (page 17)

Salt and pepper to taste

1 teaspoon (5 ml) garlic powder

Avocado Oil for cooking

Parsley, for garnish

MARINATE shrimp in Greek Vinaigrette for 30 to 45 minutes in refrigerator prior to cooking.

WHILE shrimp is marinating, bake sweet potatoes on 400° F (200° C) for 45 minutes, or microwave approximately 5 minutes and set aside to cool.

ADD avocado oil to a pan over medium-high heat. Carefully break off mushroom stems and add mushroom caps to skillet, tossing to coat. Cook approximately 5 minutes until tender. Remove from pan and set aside.

RETURN pan back to stove and add 2 tablespoons (30 ml) of avocado oil. Wrap each shrimp with ½ slice of bacon and secure with toothpick. Add to oiled pan, turning occasionally until shrimp are pink on both sides and bacon is thoroughly cooked (approximately 4 to 5 minutes on each side).

WHILE the bacon-wrapped shrimp are cooking, scoop potato flesh into a bowl and mash. Add ghee, salt, pepper, and garlic powder, and stir.

ADD sweet potato mixture to mushroom caps and top with shrimp.

GARNISH with parsley and serve immediately.

MACRONUTRIENTS: 2 PIECES PER SERVING | CALORIES: 322 | FAT: 16 G | CARB: 19 G | PROTEIN: 10 G

CHIPOTLE LIME CAULIFLOWER HUMMUS

SERVES: 6 | **PREP TIME:** 10 minutes | **COOK TIME:** 25 minutes

DAIRY FREE · KETO · WHOLE 30 *option* · NO ADDED SUGAR

Roasted cauliflower and Chipotle Lime Mayo lend a really nice and balanced flavor to this creamy hummus. Nothing too spicy or overpowering, and you still catch hints of the roasted cauliflower. Perfect snacking dip or appetizer to bring to a tailgating party.

1 head cauliflower, cut into florets

1 ¼ teaspoons (6.25 ml) sea salt

½ teaspoon (2.5 ml) smoked paprika

3 tablespoons (45 ml) Avocado Oil

2 tablespoons (30 ml) lime juice

⅓ cup (75 ml) Chipotle Lime Mayo* (page 15)

½ cup (125 ml) fresh cilantro

1 teaspoon (5 ml) garlic powder

PREHEAT oven to 400° F (200° C), and line a baking sheet with parchment paper.

CUT the florets off the cauliflower, place them on the baking sheet, and toss with avocado oil, paprika, and 1 teaspoon of salt. Roast the cauliflower for 20 to 25 minutes, or until softened and slightly browned.

ADD the roasted cauliflower, Chipotle Lime Mayo, cilantro, garlic, and remaining salt to a food processor and blend until mixture is smooth.

SERVE immediately while warm, or place in an airtight container to cool in the refrigerator.

DRIZZLE more avocado oil and paprika on top before serving, and enjoy!

*USE Primal Kitchen brand Chipotle Lime Mayo for a Whole30-approved recipe.

MACRONUTRIENTS: ½ CUP (125 ML) PER SERVING | CALORIES: 191 | FAT: 17 G | CARB: 9 G | PROTEIN: 3 G

CRISPY and CREAMY AVOCADO FRIES

SERVES: 2 | PREP TIME: 15 minutes | COOK TIME: 5 minutes

 DAIRY FREE  NO ADDED SUGAR

Before you scarf down an entire plateful, keep in mind that a little bit of crisp and cream goes a long way. Avocado fries are both rich and filling, so a small portion is plenty satisfying. This simple recipe gives avocado fries a Southwest flair, adding cumin and chili powder to the mix. You could take this theme a little further by adding finely chopped cilantro to the coating and finishing with a squirt of fresh lime.

1 avocado, pitted

½ teaspoon (2.5 ml) kosher salt

¼ teaspoon (1.25 ml) ground cumin

½ teaspoon (2.5 ml) chili powder

½ cup (125 ml) unsweetened coconut flakes

¼ cup (60 ml) coconut flour

1 egg, whisked

Avocado Oil for frying

Chipotle Lime Mayo (page 15) for dipping

HALVE the avocado and remove the pit. Slice it into eight wedges and remove the peel.

SPRINKLE the wedges with ¼ teaspoon (1.25 ml) of salt, making sure to lightly coat all sides.

IN a food processor, blend the remaining ¼ teaspoon (1.25 ml) salt, cumin, and chili powder with the coconut flakes until the coconut flakes are finely chopped.

NEAR the stove, set up an assembly line of three bowls—one for the egg, one for the coconut flour, and one for the coconut flakes.

COAT each wedge of avocado in egg, then coconut flour, and then back into the egg, followed by coconut flakes.

HEAT a thin layer of avocado oil in a deep pan over medium-high heat. When the oil is hot, add the coconut-coated avocado wedges. Fry for about 1 minute or less on the first side, or until nicely browned. Use a fork (or a fork and spoon) to turn the wedges as they brown until all sides are crispy. If the oil starts to smoke, turn down the heat.

SERVE avocado fries immediately with Chipotle Lime Mayo.

MACRONUTRIENTS: 8 FRIES PER SERVING | CALORIES: 479 | FAT: 41 G | CARB: 23 G | PROTEIN: 9 G

COBB SALAD CUPS

SERVES: 8 | PREP TIME: 15 minutes | COOK TIME: 30 minutes

 DAIRY FREE *option*   KETO

Cobb Salad Cups are a great appetizer for parties and make great side salads to add to lunches!

4 hard-boiled eggs

4 slices sugar-free bacon, chopped

3 cups (450 g) romaine lettuce, finely chopped

2 ½ tablespoons (37.5 ml) Honey Mustard Vinaigrette (page 19)

2 Roma tomatoes, diced

1 avocado, diced

4 green onions, sliced

2 cups (500 ml) shredded rotisserie or canned chicken

1 cup (250 ml) blue cheese or goat cheese* (optional)

HARD-BOIL the eggs by placing them in a pot and covering with water. Bring them to a boil, then cover, remove from heat, and let eggs sit for 10 minutes. Once done, place the eggs in a bowl of ice water to cool.

ONCE cool, peel eggs and dice into small pieces.

NEXT, add bacon to a cold skillet. Turn on stove to medium heat. Cook for about 15 minutes, flipping once halfway through. Once cooked, place on a paper towel to drain and cool.

IN a small bowl, toss together finely chopped romaine and Honey Mustard Vinaigrette.

IN desired serving cups, evenly distribute and layer eggs, romaine lettuce, diced tomatoes, chicken, avocado, blue cheese, bacon, and green onions.

SERVE immediately.

*OMIT cheese for a dairy-free recipe

MACRONUTRIENTS: 1 SALAD PER SERVING | CALORIES: 273 | FAT: 20 G | CARB: 5 G | PROTEIN: 18 G

BBQ CHICKEN DIP

SERVES: 5 to 6 | **PREP TIME:** 15 minutes | **COOK TIME:** 50 minutes

 DAIRY FREE

This BBQ Chicken Dip combines all of your favorite BBQ chicken pizza flavors into a delicious dip perfect for gameday watch parties or backyard barbecues. Have a favorite paleo BBQ sauce? Feel free to swap in 1 ½ cups to simplify the recipe even more!

2 cups (500 ml) shredded rotisserie or canned chicken

½ cup (125 ml) raw cashews

½ cup (125 ml) Classic Mayo (page 13)

⅓ cup (75 ml) red onion, diced

3 tablespoons (45 ml) cilantro, minced, plus more for garnish

1 cup (250 ml) BBQ Sauce (page 33)

HEAT oven to 350° F (180° C) degrees.

BOIL cashews in 2 cups of water for 30 minutes.

ONCE cashews are done, place cashews and ¼ cup (60 ml) cooking liquid into your blender and mix until smooth.

FOLD in cashew cream with shredded chicken, BBQ sauce, mayo, red onion, and cilantro.

PLACE into small casserole dish or large ramekin.

COOK for 20 minutes until top is a little crusty.

TOP with more cilantro and serve with celery sticks or carrots.

MACRONUTRIENTS: ½ (125 ML) CUP PER SERVING | CALORIES: 412 | FAT: 33 G | CARB: 13 G | PROTEIN: 17 G

VEGGIE SUSHI

SERVES: 3 | PREP TIME: 30 minutes | COOK TIME: 8 minutes

 DAIRY FREE WHOLE 30 *option* NO ADDED SUGAR

Who says eating your vegetables can't be fun! The mayo double duties for function (it acts as a glue for the cauliflower rice) and adds great flavor.

1 head cauliflower	1 English cucumber, thinly sliced
⅓ cup (75 ml) Chipotle Lime Mayo* (page 15)	1 avocado, pitted
1 red pepper, thinly sliced	2 cups (300 g) micro greens
1 yellow pepper, thinly sliced	6 nori sheets
1 mango, thinly sliced	1 tablespoon (15 ml) Avocado Oil

REMOVE the cauliflower florets, rinse, and pat dry. Rice the cauliflower in a food processor using the grater attachment, or by hand using a box grater.

HEAT avocado oil in a large skillet over medium heat. Add the riced cauliflower, give it a quick toss to coat, then cover with a lid so the cauliflower steams and becomes tender, about 6 to 8 minutes.

IN a large bowl, mix the riced cauliflower with Chipotle Lime Mayo.

LAY a sheet of nori on the sushi rolling mat and start to scoop and spread the cauliflower rice onto the nori. You'll want to cover the nori from edge to edge with a thin, even layer of rice, but leave a 1-inch space at one end of the nori without rice.

ADD your fillings, placing them close to the end of the nori where the rice comes all the way to the edge. Lay the pieces in a thin row, and try not to add too much filling, as doing so will make it harder to roll.

NOW you're ready to start rolling your sushi. Grab a small bowl or glass of water to keep on hand. Place the sushi mat so that the side of the nori with the filling is facing you. Start to roll by pulling up the mat slightly and tucking the row of filling into the first complete roll. Press down with the mat around the now tucked row of filling to help make a nice tight roll. Continue rolling with the help of the mat, pressing/tucking as you go to keep the roll tight until you get to the end of the nori sheet (with the 1-inch section without rice). Dab a bit of water on the end of the nori to help it stick to itself, and then complete your final roll.

USING a clean, sharp knife, cut the sushi into pieces. If your ends are looking a little messy, you can trim these off first for a nice clean edge. It also helps to wipe off your knife after every one to two slices so that you keep the cuts clean and without bits of cauliflower rice getting onto the nori.

SERVE immediately.

'USE Primal Kitchen brand Chipotle Lime Mayo for a Whole30-approved recipe.

"I think people tend to overcomplicate cooking and become overwhelmed.
My rule in the kitchen is there are no rules. If a recipe calls for garlic,
and you don't like garlic, simply leave it out. Cooking can be as simple
and cheap or as complicated and expensive as you want it to be.
You are the master of your dish."

– Vevian Vozmediano, Fitalicious Life

CHIPOTLE BACON DEVILED EGGS

SERVES: 8 | **PREP TIME:** 15 minutes | **COOK TIME:** 25 minutes

 DAIRY FREE KETO WHOLE 30 *option* NO ADDED SUGAR

With minimal ingredients, these deviled eggs are as simple to make as they are delicious!

8 eggs

⅓ cup (75 ml) Chipotle Lime Mayo*
(page 15)

2 slices sugar-free bacon

1 to 2 teaspoons (5 to 10 ml) of paprika,
for garnish (optional)

HARD-BOIL the eggs by placing them in a pot and covering with water. Bring them to a boil, then cover, remove from heat, and let eggs sit for 10 minutes. Once done, place the eggs in a bowl of ice water to cool.

WHILE the eggs are cooling, add bacon to a cold skillet. Turn on stove to medium heat. Cook for about 15 minutes, flipping once halfway through. Once cooked, place on a paper towel to drain and cool.

NOW that the eggs are cool, peel them carefully and slice lengthwise.

BEING sure not to disrupt the egg whites, carefully remove the yolks and place into a large mixing bowl.

WITH a fork, break up the egg yolks until they are the texture of a moist powder.

DICE the bacon and add most of it (save some for garnish), along with the mayo, to the yolks. Mix well to combine.

ONCE fully combined, scoop about 2 teaspoons (10 ml) of egg yolk mixture back into the eggs.

IF you have a piping bag and want your eggs to look super fancy, feel free to use it, but it isn't necessary.

ONCE all the eggs are full, add the remaining diced bacon as a garnish, plus a bit of paprika.

*USE Primal Kitchen brand Chipotle Lime Mayo for a Whole30-approved recipe.

MACRONUTRIENTS: 2 EGGS PER SERVING | CALORIES: 194 | FAT: 17 G | CARB: 2 G | PROTEIN: 7 G

BUFFALO CHICKEN
JALAPEÑO POPPERS

SERVES: 8 | **PREP TIME:** 15 minutes | **COOK TIME:** 45 minutes

 DAIRY FREE KETO  *option*  NO ADDED SUGAR

These Buffalo Chicken Jalapeño Poppers combine all the goodness of buffalo wings into a bite-sized jalapeño popper. A crumble of pork rinds gives these jalapeño poppers the perfect extra crunch. These savory and spicy bites are great served with other healthy appetizers when cheering on your favorite sports team!

¼ cup (60 ml) raw cashews

8 jalapeños

¼ cup (60 ml) Classic Mayo (page 13)

¼ cup (60 ml) hot sauce*

5 oz (142 g) canned chicken, drained and shredded

½ cup (125 ml) crushed pork rinds*

PREHEAT oven to 400° F (200° C).

BOIL cashews in 2 cups of water for 30 minutes.

WHILE cashews are cooking, cut jalapeños in half lengthwise and deseed.

ONCE cashews are done, place them into your blender with 2 tablespoons of cooking liquid, plus mayo and hot sauce, and blend until smooth.

POUR the sauce into a bowl with shredded chicken, and mix until fully combined.

SCOOP the buffalo chicken into jalapeño cavities. Top with crushed pork rinds.

PLACE on a baking sheet and bake for 15 minutes.

SERVE immediately.

*USE a Whole30 Approved hot sauce and omit pork rinds for a Whole30-approved recipe.

MACRONUTRIENTS: 2 POPPERS PER SERVING | CALORIES: 228 | FAT: 22 G | CARB: 2 G | PROTEIN: 6 G

BUTTER LETTUCE
SHRIMP TACOS

SERVES: 3 to 4 | **PREP TIME:** 15 minutes | **COOK TIME:** 5 minutes

 DAIRY FREE   WHOLE 30  NO ADDED SUGAR

This is not your average Taco Tuesday! These butter lettuce-wrapped shrimp tacos are sure to be a crowd pleaser. This yummy recipe can be served as an appetizer or paired with your favorite sides for a meal.

¼ cup (60 ml) Classic Mayo (page 13)

1 pound (455 g) raw, wild-caught, cleaned shrimp

2 tablespoons (30 ml) Avocado Oil

4 cups (½ medium head) cabbage, shredded

2 limes

1 avocado, pitted

¼ cup (60 ml) cilantro

1 head butter lettuce

1 tablespoon (15 ml) paprika

½ tablespoon (7.5 ml) ground cumin

1 tablespoon (15 ml) chili powder

½ tablespoon (7.5 ml) garlic powder

½ tablespoon (7.5 ml) onion powder

¼ to ½ tablespoon (3.75 to 7.5 ml) crushed red pepper

MIX taco seasoning ingredients (paprika, cumin, chili, garlic, and onion powders) together in a small bowl.

COAT the raw shrimp in the taco seasoning; then sauté in avocado oil over medium-high heat until fully cooked (about 5 minutes), flipping as needed.

IN a large bowl, mix the mayo with the juice of one lime, and whisk until thin. Toss the shredded cabbage in the mix to coat.

PLACE the butter lettuce wraps on a plate and layer the shrimp, cabbage slaw, avocado, and cilantro respectively. Squeeze lime juice over the tacos.

SERVE immediately.

MACRONUTRIENTS: 2 TACOS PER SERVING | CALORIES: 443 | FAT: 30 G | CARB: 20 G | PROTEIN: 30 G

SIDES

Side dishes can make or break a meal. Your sides shouldn't play second fiddle to the main course, and deserve a standing ovation all of their own. This chapter is full of tantalizing and healthful creative trimmings. Sides just got sizzle!

SUNCHOKE SALAD

SERVES: 4 | **PREP TIME:** 5 minutes | **COOK TIME:** 5 minutes

 DAIRY FREE

This is a spicy take on a traditional potato salad. The only changes you will notice involve sunchokes (also called Jerusalem artichokes) in place of potatoes, and Chipotle Lime Mayo in place of the more pedestrian varieties we grew up with.

1 cup (250 ml) Chipotle Lime Mayo (page 15)

2 tablespoons (30 ml) apple cider vinegar

1 ½ teaspoon (7.5 ml) sea salt

1 teaspoon (5 ml) honey

½ teaspoon (2.5 ml) black pepper

4 cups (1000 ml) sunchokes, cubed

1 cup (250 ml) celery, diced

½ cup (125 ml) red onion, finely chopped

2 hard-boiled eggs, diced

PREP the sunchokes just like a potato: wash, cut out eyes, and then chop into 1-inch cubes.

BRING a large pot of water to boil over high heat. Boil sunchokes for about 5 to 8 minutes.

WHEN the sunchokes are tender, strain them and allow to cool.

WHILE the sunchokes are cooling, combine the first five ingredients into a large mixing bowl and set aside.

ONCE cooled, add sunchokes, celery, red onion, and hard-boiled eggs to the sauce mixture.

TOSS to evenly coat with sauce and serve immediately, or store in an airtight container.

MACRONUTRIENTS: 1 CUP PER SERVING | CALORIES: 585 | FAT: 47 G | CARB: 36 G | PROTEIN: 8 G

CHIPOTLE LIME ROASTED
BROCCOLI and CAULIFLOWER

SERVES: 4 to 6 | **PREP TIME:** 15 minutes | **COOK TIME:** 30 minutes

 DAIRY FREE KETO  WHOLE 30 *option*  NO ADDED SUGAR

You know what makes French fries so irresistible? Fat, salt, and crunch. That's what makes these veggies so irresistible too. And since this recipe is made with avocado oil, a super-healthy good-for-you fat, there's nothing to feel guilty about!

1 head broccoli

1 head cauliflower

½ cup (125 ml) Chipotle Lime Mayo*
  (page 15)

¼ cup (60 ml) Avocado Oil

½ teaspoon (2.5 ml) sea salt

Radishes, for garnish (optional)

Grape tomatoes, for garnish (optional)

SET the oven to 400° F (200° C) and line a baking sheet with parchment paper. Set aside.

CUT the broccoli and cauliflower into large pieces.

MIX the Chipotle Lime Mayo, avocado oil, and sea salt in a mixing bowl, and then use a silicone basting brush to apply the mixture to the tops of each piece. Place the cauliflower topside down, and the broccoli topside up.

BAKE for 10 minutes, then remove the sheet from the oven and flip the broccoli topside down. (You can put the broccoli topside down from the beginning, but it browns much faster, and it may burn.)

BAKE for another 20 minutes.

GARNISH with radishes and grape tomatoes if desired and serve immediately.

*USE Primal Kitchen brand Chipotle Lime Mayo for a Whole30-approved recipe.

MACRONUTRIENTS: 1 CUP PER SERVING | CALORIES: 347 | FAT: 29 G | CARB: 19 G | PROTEIN: 7 G

LOADED POTATO WEDGES

SERVES: 6 | **PREP TIME:** 15 minutes | **COOK TIME:** 50 minutes

 DAIRY FREE *option*   KETO   NO ADDED SUGAR

These loaded potato wedges are topped with bacon, goat cheese, pickled onions, cilantro, avocado, and a creamy hot sauce. Perfect for a large group or on game day!

2 pounds (900 g) Yukon Gold potatoes

3 tablespoons (45 ml) Avocado Oil

1 teaspoon (5 ml) chili powder

1 teaspoon (5 ml) granulated garlic

1 teaspoon (5 ml) sea salt

¼ cup (60 ml) Chipotle Lime Mayo (page 15)

⅓ cup (75 ml) Buffalo or wing sauce

5 ounces (113 g) goat cheese* (optional)

1 pound (455 g) sugar-free bacon, chopped

¼ cup (60 ml) fresh cilantro, chopped

½ cup (125 ml) pickled onions

1 avocado, sliced

PREHEAT oven to 400° F (200° C) and line a baking sheet with parchment paper.

CUT the potatoes in half lengthwise, then cut those halves lengthwise, and then repeat one more time. You can slice in half an additional time if you want even smaller wedges.

TOSS the wedges with the avocado oil, chili powder, garlic, and sea salt.

PLACE the wedges in a single layer on the baking sheet and cook for 25 minutes. Rotate the pan and cook for another 20 to 25 minutes, or until potatoes are cooked through and crispy.

WHILE the potatoes are cooking, mix together the Chipotle Lime Mayo and Buffalo sauce and set aside.

COOK the bacon in a skillet over medium-high heat until it's crispy. Let it cool, and then chop into small pieces.

WHEN the potatoes are done cooking, place them on a large tray or plate. Top with goat cheese, bacon, cilantro, pickled onions, and avocado, and then drizzle on the hot sauce mixture right before serving.

*OMIT cheese for a dairy-free recipe.

MACRONUTRIENTS: 4 WEDGES PER SERVING | CALORIES: 584 | FAT: 45 G | CARB: 7 G | PROTEIN: 17 G

FRENCH ONION SOUP GRATINÉE

SERVES: 1 to 2 | **PREP TIME:** 15 minutes | **COOK TIME:** 1 hour 20 minutes

 KETO    NO ADDED SUGAR

This is a great take on a delicious, classic soup. This recipe is gluten free and more nutrient dense thanks to the use of collagen-rich beef bone broth. (Note: if you have digestive issues, like SIBO or IBS, do a 14Four.me diet reset first to determine if you tolerate cheese before adding this soup to your menu plan.)

- 4 to 5 cups (4 medium) onions, sliced thinly into "rainbows" or half circles
- 2 tablespoons (30 ml) Avocado Oil
- 1 ½ cups (375 ml) beef broth
- 1 teaspoon (5 ml) fresh thyme
- Salt and pepper to taste
- 5 ounces (141 g) Gruyère cheese, grated or very thinly sliced

HEAT the oil in a large pot over medium heat. Add the onions and cook, stirring, until they reduce from their original size of 5 cups (670 g) to a final 1 cup (150 g) cooked onions.

TOWARD the end of cooking time (30 minutes to an hour depending on the pot and heat), stir more frequently. You want some browning of the onions, but not burning, which will turn the taste bitter.

ADD the broth and use a wooden spoon to scrape up brown bits from the bottom of the pan (called deglazing).

NOTE: If you would like to use some red wine, traditionally used to add depth to French onion soup, replace ½ cup (125 ml) of the broth with wine and add it in first, cooking for 5 minutes before adding the broth.

ADD the thyme, salt, and pepper, stir, and bring to a simmer. Cook for 5 minutes, or if using alcohol, 10 minutes to make sure the alcohol cooks out.

IF you have ramekins, preheat the oven. Ramekins are little ceramic bowls that can be heated in the oven. If you don't have ramekins, don't worry, just add the Gruyère to the soup and heat it thoroughly for 5 minutes or so until it is melted inside the soup. Then serve. If using ramekins, ladle the soup into one 2-cup ramekin or two 1-cup ramekins.

COVER the top of the soup with the Gruyère cheese and place ramekin(s) on a tray. Cook in the oven for 10 minutes, and if you'd like, finish with 1 to 2 minutes under the broiler.

SERVE immediately.

MACRONUTRIENTS: 1 ½ CUPS PER SERVING | CALORIES: 793 | FAT: 59 G | CARB: 33 G | PROTEIN: 35 G

"For 77,000 generations, we lived in sync with our natural environment
and were remarkably lean, fit, and free of the chronic diseases that have become
epidemic today: obesity, diabetes, heart disease, Alzheimer's, and autoimmune disease.

Unfortunately, our modern environment—our diet, lifestyle, air, water,
and social matrix—has changed much faster than our bodies have been able to adapt.

This mismatch between our genes and biology on the one hand, and
our modern environment on the other, is driving the dramatic increase in
chronic disease, shortening our lifespan, and destroying our quality of life.

Following a paleo or 'primal' approach is the best way to realign your diet and lifestyle
with the natural human template—and thus prevent and reverse modern disease."

—Chris Kresser, M.S., L.Ac.

BACON BROCCOLI SALAD

SERVES: 4 | **PREP TIME:** 45 minutes

DAIRY FREE · KETO · WHOLE 30 *option* · NO ADDED SUGAR *option*

Nothing beats the crunch and tang of this perfectly balanced salad. Nutrient dense and full of healthy fat, this dish will be a hit at a weekend picnic or as a weeknight dinner side. Pairs well with chicken.

12 ounces (340 g) broccoli florets, cut to uniform size

¼ cup (60 ml) grape tomatoes, cut into thirds

¼ cup (60 ml) goji berries

¼ cup (60 ml) sprouted sunflower seeds

4 slices sugar-free bacon chopped

⅓ cup (75 ml) Classic Mayo (page 13)

1 tablespoon (15 ml) apple cider vinegar

1 tablespoon (15 ml) MCT oil

1 tablespoon (15 ml) shallot, minced

1 teaspoon (5 ml) raw honey* (optional)

Salt and pepper to taste

IN a medium bowl, mix together the broccoli, tomatoes, goji berries, sunflower seeds, and bacon.

SEPARATELY, in a small bowl, combine dressing ingredients mayo, apple cider vinegar, MCT oil, shallot, and honey (if using).

WHISK mixture until combined, and then season with salt and pepper to taste.

ADD dressing to the salad and stir to ensure all broccoli is coated.

REFRIGERATE for 30 minutes to allow flavors to mingle.

*OMIT raw honey for a no-added-sugar and Whole30-approved recipe.

MACRONUTRIENTS: ¾ CUP PER SERVING | CALORIES: 328 | FAT: 29 G | CARB: 8 G | PROTEIN: 8 G

WARM CHIPOTLE LIME
SWEET POTATO SALAD

SERVES: 6 | **PREP TIME:** 30 minutes | **COOK TIME:** 30 minutes

 DAIRY FREE   KETO   WHOLE 30 *option*   NO ADDED SUGAR

Add life to your plate with this Warm Chipotle Lime Sweet Potato Salad. You're going to love the flavors that come together when you combine Chipotle Lime Mayo with sweet potatoes, sautéed veggies, and bacon. This salad is delicious and perfect for the cooler months of the year. Leftovers taste great warm or chilled!

1 ½ tablespoons (22.5 ml) ghee, divided

3 cups (4 medium) sweet potatoes, peeled and cubed

½ red onion, sliced

1 small bell pepper, diced

4 cloves garlic, minced

2 cups (300 g) kale or spinach, roughly chopped

4 slices sugar-free bacon, chopped

⅓ cup (75 ml) Chipotle Lime Mayo* (page 15)

Sea salt and black pepper to taste

ADD 1 tablespoon of ghee to a large skillet on medium-high heat. Once ghee is hot, add cubed sweet potatoes. Dash with a little sea salt and black pepper. Sauté for about 10-12 minutes, stirring throughout.

ADD the remaining ½ tablespoon (8 ml) of ghee, diced pepper, sliced onion, and garlic. Sauté for another 10 minutes. At this time, the sweet potatoes should be cooked through.

ADD chopped bacon and sauté until almost done. Add kale and cook for 2-3 minutes longer, until kale is slightly wilted and bacon is cooked until desired crispiness.

TRANSFER to a bowl (or leave in the skillet) and gently stir in the Chipotle Lime Mayo. Serve warm. Leftovers can be served warm or cold.

GARNISH with fresh parsley and green onions, if desired.

*USE Primal Kitchen brand Chipotle Lime Mayo for a Whole30-approved recipe.

MACRONUTRIENTS: 1 CUP PER SERVING | CALORIES: 250 | FAT: 18 G | CARB: 1 G | PROTEIN: 0.4 G

SPICY EGG SALAD

SERVES: 2 to 3 | **PREP TIME:** 10 minutes | **COOK TIME:** 10 minutes

 DAIRY FREE KETO WHOLE 30 *option* NO ADDED SUGAR

I loved egg salad as a child, but for some reason took a 15-year hiatus from eating it. Probably because no mayonnaise ever tasted right unless I made my own, which meant more time and dishes, so I avoided it. Eventually, I realized what I was missing. So, I started creating egg salad recipes again, and wow do they taste great! Make sure you play with flavors and add-ins to fit according to your taste buds.

6 hard-boiled eggs

½ cup (125 ml) Classic Mayo (page 13)

2 tablespoons (30 ml) hot sauce*

1 teaspoon (5 ml) black pepper

½ teaspoon (2.5 ml) fresh herbs

Salt to taste

HARD-BOIL the eggs by placing them in a pot and covering with water. Bring to a boil, then cover, remove from heat, and let eggs sit for 10 minutes. Once done, place the eggs in a bowl of ice water to cool.

NOW that the eggs are cool, peel them and place in a large bowl.

ROUGHLY chop your eggs, and then add all the remaining ingredients.

STIR well and taste test. Adjust hot sauce or seasonings to taste.

*USE Whole30 Approved hot sauce for a Whole30-approved recipe.

MACRONUTRIENTS: ½ CUP PER SERVING | CALORIES: 673 | FAT: 57 G | CARB: 3 G | PROTEIN: 35 G

MOROCCAN CARROT SALAD

SERVES: 4 | PREP TIME: 15 minutes

 DAIRY FREE KETO

Out of all the salads I've made for friends, this one has probably received the most enthusiastic response. And you can have it on the table in less than 10 minutes! The secret is in the dressing, which includes ginger and sumac. The dressing does contain a small amount of honey, so if you're trying to remove all added sugar, just omit the honey and go for a more acidic dressing.

4 tablespoons (60 ml) Primal Kitchen Extra Virgin Avocado Oil

1 tablespoon (15 ml) lemon juice

1 tablespoon (15 ml) apple cider vinegar

1 tablespoon (15 ml) honey

1 teaspoon (5 ml) fresh ginger, grated

1 long red chili, deseeded and finely chopped (optional)

½ teaspoon (2.5 ml) ground sumac

4 large carrots, grated

1 handful almonds, chopped

1 large handful cilantro, chopped

1 handful mint leaves, chopped

3 tablespoons (45 ml) dried barberries or currants

Sea salt and freshly ground black pepper

IN a large serving bowl, whisk together the avocado oil, lemon juice, vinegar, honey, and ginger until well combined.

ADD the chili, sumac, carrot, almonds, cilantro, mint, and barberries or currants. Toss, season with salt and pepper, and serve alongside your favorite protein or as part of a spread of salads at a barbecue.

MACRONUTRIENTS: 1 CUP PER SERVING | CALORIES: 432 | FAT: 33 G | CARB: 3 G | PROTEIN: 10 G

DILL PICKLE and BACON POTATO SALAD

SERVES: 6 to 8 | **PREP TIME:** 15 minutes | **COOK TIME:** 20 minutes

 DAIRY FREE *option*   WHOLE 30 *option*    NO ADDED SUGAR

Score points with this Dill Pickle and Bacon Potato Salad—the perfect party side dish!

2 pounds (900 g) russet potatoes

8 ounces (225 g) sugar-free bacon

½ cup (125 ml) cubed grass-fed Colby or cheddar cheese* (optional)

1 cup (250 ml) sliced pickles*

⅔ cups (150 ml) Classic Mayo (page 13)

2 tablespoons (30 ml) bacon fat

2 tablespoons (30 ml) pickle juice*

1 tablespoon (15 ml) Dijon Mustard* (page 39)

1 tablespoon (15 ml) fresh dill, chopped

3 garlic cloves, minced

1 ½ teaspoons (7.5 ml) salt, divided

¼ teaspoon (1.25 ml) black pepper

WASH and scrub potatoes. Cut into 1-inch (2.5 cm) bite-size pieces and add to a large pot. Cover potatoes with water and add ¾ teaspoon (3.75 ml) of salt. Bring water to a boil, reduce to simmer for 10 minutes until potatoes are fork tender, strain, and let cool for 10 minutes.

MEANWHILE, chop the uncooked bacon into small ½-inch (1 cm) bite-size pieces and add to a pan at medium heat.

COOK bacon until desired doneness, remove from pan, and let sit on a paper towel-lined plate. Be sure to save the bacon fat.

IN a large bowl, mix together mayo, bacon fat, pickle juice, mustard, chopped dill, minced garlic cloves, and ¾ teaspoons (3.75 ml) of salt and pepper.

ADD pickle slices, cheese cubes, and bacon to the sauce, and mix well.

ADD potatoes to bowl and toss to evenly coat with the sauce.

SERVE immediately, or store in an airtight container.

*OMIT cheese for a dairy-free recipe. Use Whole30 Approved pickles, pickle juice and Dijon mustard (if using store bought) for a Whole30-approved recipe.

MACRONUTRIENTS: ½ CUP PER SERVING | CALORIES: 390 | FAT: 31 G | CARB: 22 G | PROTEIN: 10 G

CREAMY CHIPOTLE
BUTTERNUT SQUASH SOUP

SERVES: 6 | PREP TIME: 20 minutes | COOK TIME: 1 hour 15 minutes

 DAIRY FREE  *option*  NO ADDED SUGAR

A soup full of creamy goodness without the cream! The Chipotle Lime Mayo adds just the right amount of heat to make this some serious comfort food.

1 large butternut squash

1 yellow onion, diced

5 to 6 cloves of garlic, minced

4 tablespoons (60 ml) Chipotle Lime Mayo* (page 15)

½ tablespoon (7.5 ml) sugar-free bacon fat

¼ teaspoon (1.25 ml) cinnamon

¼ teaspoon (1.25 ml) nutmeg

4 cups (1000 ml) chicken/beef broth

1 tablespoon (15 ml) ghee

Salt and pepper to taste

Avocado Oil to cook veggies

Roasted pumpkin seeds, for garnish

Coconut milk, for garnish

PREHEAT oven to 400° F (200° C). Line a baking sheet with parchment paper. Place a damp towel under the cutting board to stabilize it while you slice squash in half lengthwise. (Be very careful when doing this!) Scoop out the seeds. Pierce the squash all over the outside with a fork, and then coat the flesh with oil. Lay flesh-side up on the baking sheet and bake for 50-60 minutes until soft. Set aside to cool.

FILL a frying pan with enough avocado oil to coat, add diced onion and minced garlic, and cook until soft and fragrant. Set aside.

ADD 4 cups (1000 ml) of broth to a blender. (I used a Vitamix® with a hot soup setting.) Scoop out cooled flesh from squash and add to blender, along with the cooked onion and garlic, Chipotle Lime Mayo, ghee, bacon fat, and spices, and then purée until smooth. Season with salt and pepper to taste, and then blend for a bit longer to mix. If you don't have a Vitamix or Blendtec® with a soup setting, pour the soup into a large pot and cook until hot and ready to serve. Garnish with roasted pumpkin seeds and a drizzle of coconut milk. So tasty!

*USE Primal Kitchen brand Chipotle Lime Mayo for a Whole30-approved recipe.

MACRONUTRIENTS: 1 CUP PER SERVING | CALORIES: 141 | FAT: 8 G | CARB: 13 G | PROTEIN: 5 G

CURRIED CHICKEN SALAD

SERVES: 5 to 6 | **PREP TIME:** 10 minutes | **COOK TIME:** 20 minutes

 DAIRY FREE · KETO · WHOLE 30 *option* · NO ADDED SUGAR

I've always loved curried chicken salads. Such a flavorful blend of ingredients! There's sweetness from raisins, and crunch from cashews and celery. And, of course, Classic Mayo adds that all-important creaminess to the dish. This recipe is really easy to make. Whip up a large batch to store in the fridge for a few days to eat for lunch or as a quick snack.

2 chicken breasts, diced

Avocado Oil

½ cup (125 ml) green onion, diced

2 stalks celery, diced

¼ cup (60 ml) cashews or almonds

¼ cup (60 ml) raisins or currants*

½ cup (125 ml) Classic Mayo (page 13)

1 tablespoon (15 ml) curry powder

Salt to taste

Juice from ½ lemon

SAUTÉ the diced chicken in avocado oil until cooked.

AFTER the chicken has cooled, combine all the ingredients together in a large mixing bowl.

*USE Whole30 Approved raisins or currants (dried fruit commonly contains sulfites) or omit for a Whole30-approved recipe.

MACRONUTRIENTS: ½ CUP PER SERVING | CALORIES: 380 | FAT: 23 G | CARB: 10 G | PROTEIN: 34 G

ROSEMARY AIOLI
and KALEIDOSCOPE FRIES

SERVES: 3 | **PREP TIME:** 15 minutes | **COOK TIME:** 30 minutes

 DAIRY FREE  NO ADDED SUGAR

I've always been a mayo and fries kind of gal. This recipe transforms my favorite combo into a gourmet snacking experience. Dream big! Try a variety of roots and tubers like cassava, taro, parsnips, or jicama.

1 medium yam

1 medium purple potato

1 medium white sweet potato

Avocado Oil for frying

Salt and pepper to taste

½ cup (125 ml) Classic Mayo (page 13)

1 garlic clove, minced

1 teaspoon (5 ml) fresh rosemary, finely minced

1 tablespoon (15 ml) lemon juice, freshly squeezed

Salt and pepper to taste

TO make the Rosemary Aioli, combine mayo, garlic, rosemary and lemon juice together in a small bowl and stir until well combined. Add salt and pepper to taste. Store Rosemary Aioli in the refrigerator while you prepare the fries.

PEEL and slice tubers lengthwise into ¼-inch pieces; then rinse in cold water to remove any excess starch.

HEAT ⅓ to ½-inch of avocado oil in a skillet over low-medium heat. Add tubers in a single layer to the skillet and fry for 15 minutes, or until softened.

REMOVE tubers from the oil and place onto a paper towel. You'll likely need to do this in multiple batches depending upon the size of your tubers and skillet.

ONCE all tubers have been precooked, increase the heat to medium-high and fry until golden brown. This process will result in perfectly crispy fries.

SEASON fries with salt and pepper to taste. Serve immediately with Rosemary Aioli.

MACRONUTRIENTS: ⅔ CUP PER SERVING | CALORIES: 435 | FAT: 33 G | CARB: 33 G | PROTEIN: 3 G

CAVEMAN COLESLAW

SERVES: 6 to 7 | **PREP TIME:** 15 minutes

 DAIRY FREE   WHOLE 30 *option*   NO ADDED SUGAR

One of my favorite things about living a paleo lifestyle has been realizing how delicious the simple ingredients and recipes truly are. As a husband, father, and doggy dad, time is very important to me, but I never want to sacrifice my health or flavors for convenience sake. Featuring high-quality ingredients like Classic Mayo and some delicious vegetables, this coleslaw hits a home run. Adding the cranberries satisfies my sweet tooth without sparking my guilt. Enjoy!

3 cups (⅓ medium head) cabbage, shredded

2 cups (¼ medium head) red cabbage, shredded

1 cup (250 ml) shredded carrots

1 cup (250 ml) cranberries*

1 cup (250 ml) Classic Mayo (page 13)

ADD cabbage, red cabbage, carrots, and cranberries to a large mixing bowl and toss well.

ADD Classic Mayo and mix.

*USE Whole30 Approved cranberries (dried fruit commonly contains sulfites and cranberries must be sweetened with apple juice) or omit for a Whole30-approved recipe.

MACRONUTRIENTS: 1 CUP PER SERVING | CALORIES: 224 | FAT: 14 G | CARB: 25 G | PROTEIN: 1 G

TOMATO CUCUMBER SALAD

SERVES: 2 TO 4 | **PREP TIME:** 15 minutes

VEGAN DAIRY FREE KETO WHOLE30 NO ADDED SUGAR

When tomatoes are in season, this simple salad tastes exquisite. Farm-fresh produce always enhances flavors! But don't worry if they're out of season, the recipe will still taste good.

4 tomatoes on the vine	1 handful fresh basil, sliced
1 cucumber	Coarse-ground sea salt to taste
¼ onion, minced	Greek Vinaigrette (page 17) to taste

RINSE tomatoes, remove the stem, and chop into large chunks. Add tomatoes to a medium-sized mixing bowl.

CUT the cucumber in half lengthwise, and then slice each half into chunks.

ADD the chunked cucumber to the tomatoes in the bowl, along with minced onion and sliced fresh basil.

DRIZZLE Greek Vinaigrette over the entire bowl and season with sea salt to taste.

TOSS ingredients, and taste to determine if more dressing or sea salt is necessary.

SERVE alongside a main dish, or as lunch.

NOTE: While 58 percent of the calories come from carbs in this recipe, way above the keto cutoff of around 15 percent, it still earns the keto icon because it's so few total calories. You can consume high-fiber, high-water-content vegetables (like those in this recipe) liberally and still stay keto aligned.

MACRONUTRIENTS: 1 CUP PER SERVING | CALORIES: 89 | FAT: 27 G | CARB: 13 G | PROTEIN: 3 G

DUCHESS SWEET POTATOES

SERVES: 3 | **PREP TIME:** 25 minutes | **COOK TIME:** 40 minutes

 DAIRY FREE  NO ADDED SUGAR

Elegant, yet oh-so-simple to prepare, these tasty beauties are sure to become your favorite potato side dish.

1 pound (455 g) Hannah sweet potatoes

1 teaspoon (5 ml) Himalayan pink salt

¼ teaspoon (1.25 ml) nutmeg

½ cup (125 ml) Classic Mayo (page 13)

PEEL sweet potatoes and cut into 1-inch (2.5 cm) cubes. Place in a pot and fill with just enough water to cover. Simmer for about 15 minutes, or until soft when pierced with a fork.

DRAIN potatoes and place in a bowl with Classic Mayo, salt, and nutmeg. Blend until very smooth.

FILL a star-tipped pastry bag with the potato mixture. Pipe out 3-inch circles onto a parchment-lined baking sheet. Place in refrigerator for at least 30 minutes.

PREHEAT oven to 400°F (200° C). Bake potatoes on the middle rack for 15 minutes. Rotate and bake another 10 minutes, or until golden.

MACRONUTRIENTS: 2 POTATOES PER SERVING | CALORIES: 367 | FAT: 28 G | CARB: 27 G | PROTEIN: 2 G

CREAMY
ROASTED TOMATO SOUP

SERVES: 6 | **PREP TIME:** 30 minutes | **COOK TIME:** 60 minutes

 VEGAN    DAIRY FREE   KETO   WHOLE 30    NO ADDED SUGAR

Sometimes the perfect cup of soup not only hits the spot in your belly, but also in your heart. It's like a warm hug in a bowl. It's like a snuggly blanket fresh out of the dryer. It's like cuddling with your adorable puppy. OK, that's plenty of soup analogies...you get the picture. This is by far my favorite soup to make on days when it's a little chilly, or if I just want some serious comfort food.

- 6 large tomatoes
- 3 garlic cloves
- A handful of basil
- 4 tablespoons (60 ml) Primal Kitchen Extra Virgin Avocado Oil
- Salt and pepper to taste
- 2 jalapeños or serrano chilies (optional)

PREHEAT oven to 375° F (190° C).

CHOP tomatoes, garlic, and basil, and place in an oven-safe baking dish.

DRIZZLE the chopped veggies with extra-virgin avocado oil and salt and pepper.

COVER baking dish with foil and bake for 1 hour.

REMOVE the tomatoes from the oven very carefully; the dish will be full of boiling liquid that you can't see beneath the foil.

ALLOW tomatoes to cool for 15 or 20 minutes to make them easier to handle.

POUR tomatoes and all contents of the dish into a blender and blend until liquid is smooth.

EAT immediately, and refrigerate/freeze remaining soup in single-serving, reusable containers for easily reheatable meals.

MACRONUTRIENTS: 1 CUP PER SERVING | CALORIES: 119 | FAT: 10 G | CARB: 8 G | PROTEIN: 2 G

MUSTARD BRUSSELS SPROUTS
with **LEEKS**

SERVES: 6 to 8 | **PREP TIME:** 15 minutes | **COOK TIME:** 15 minutes

 DAIRY FREE

Brussels sprouts, bacon, and mustard! A classic, delectable combination has never been easier to make. Shredded Brussels sprouts spiked with Honey Mustard Vinaigrette and stuffed with crispy bacon makes for an enjoyable, crispy cruciferous veggie!

8 cups (800 g) Brussels sprouts

1 large leek

2 slices bacon

2 teaspoons (10 ml) sea salt

1 teaspoons (5 ml) black pepper

⅓ cup (75 ml) Honey Mustard Vinaigrette (page 19)

SLICE the Brussels sprouts into ⅛-inch slices to shred, starting at the bottom.

SLICE the leek lengthwise, rinse the inside thoroughly, shake dry, and then cut in ⅛-inch slices.

CHOP the bacon into ¼-inch pieces. Heat a large cast iron skillet on medium-high heat.

ADD in the bacon pieces and cook, stirring often until browned, about 3 minutes.

ADD the leek slices to the skillet and stir to break apart. Sauté until tender, about 3 to 4 minutes. Next add in 4 to 5 (675 g) cups of the shredded Brussels sprouts.

BRING the heat up to high.

STIR in the salt and pepper. Cook the Brussels sprouts on high for 4 minutes, stirring occasionally.

AROUND the 4-minute mark you'll begin to notice little bits beginning to char!

ADD in the Honey Mustard Vinaigrette and cook, stirring often, for another 3 to 4 minutes.

MACRONUTRIENTS: 1 CUP PER SERVING | CALORIES: 131 | FAT: 8 G | CARB: 12 G | PROTEIN: 4 G

Sébastien Noël, Paleo Leap

ZESTY GREEK
SWEET POTATOES

SERVES: 4 | PREP TIME: 15 minutes | COOK TIME: 25 minutes

 VEGAN  DAIRY FREE WHOLE 30  NO ADDED SUGAR

These Greek-seasoned sweet potatoes are a perfect go-to side dish. The minimal prep will save you time on busy evenings. Just make sure to keep some Greek Vinaigrette on hand. They also pair well with any protein, making this tasty side dish even more versatile.

4 sweet potatoes, peeled and chopped into 1-inch cubes

½ cup (125 ml) onion, diced

1 garlic clove, minced

¼ cup (60 ml) Greek Vinaigrette (page 17)

Sea salt and freshly ground pepper

PREHEAT oven to 375º F (190° C).

PLACE sweet potatoes, onion, garlic, and vinaigrette in a large bowl.

SEASON to taste with salt and pepper, and then toss to coat.

SPREAD into a single layer on a baking sheet.

BAKE in the oven for 25 to 30 minutes, until sweet potatoes are tender, stirring halfway through.

REMOVE from oven and serve warm.

MACRONUTRIENTS: 1 CUP PER SERVING | CALORIES: 209 | FAT: 80 G | CARB: 29 G | PROTEIN: 2 G

CHIPOTLE CREAMED SPINACH

SERVES: 4 | **PREP TIME:** 5 minutes | **COOK TIME:** 5 minutes

 DAIRY FREE   KETO    WHOLE 30 *option*   NO ADDED SUGAR

Can I be honest here? I used to hate all kinds of cooked spinach. I couldn't do it—the consistency, the flavor, none of it. A couple years ago, I was hiking in Arizona and stumbled upon this tastebud-blowingly-amazing restaurant, which totally changed my feelings on cooked spinach forever. But I couldn't handle the dairy, so when I got home, I made a dairy-free version with mayonnaise instead of heavy cream! Heck to the yesss.

6 heaping cups (900 g) fresh spinach

½ cup (125 ml) Chipotle Lime Mayo* (page 15)

2 tablespoons (30 ml) chicken broth

1 tablespoon (15 ml) lime juice

½ teaspoon (2.5 ml) garlic, minced

¼ teaspoon (1.25 ml) cumin

¼ teaspoon (1.25 ml) chipotle powder

½ teaspoon (2.5 ml) sea salt

COMBINE the mayo, chicken broth, lime juice, garlic, cumin, chipotle powder, and sea salt in a small bowl or measuring cup. Mix until the ingredients are well combined.

HEAT a large skillet over medium heat and pour in the mayo mixture. Cook over medium heat until bubbles begin to appear, about 2 to 3 minutes, stirring every so often with a wooden spoon.

ADD the spinach into the skillet, distributing evenly. Turn the heat to medium low.

PUT a lid on the skillet and cook until the spinach starts to wilt, about 3 to 5 minutes. Remove the lid and mix the spinach so it is coated in the sauce. At this point, the spinach will be cooked through, but not completely wilted.

REMOVE from heat and serve immediately.

SERVE with any Mexican or Southwestern-inspired dishes, or on a bed of cauliflower rice. It's great with plantain chips too.

*USE Primal Kitchen brand Chipotle Lime Mayo for a Whole30-approved recipe.

MACRONUTRIENTS: ½ CUP PER SERVING | CALORIES: 223 | FAT: 22 G | CARB: 5 G | PROTEIN: 2 G

MAIN DISHES

From meat to fish to fowl—we've got you covered for every dinner occasion and palate. Whether you're dining alone, as a couple, or entertaining an entire dinner party, these dishes aim to please. And remember, making a little extra at dinner leaves you with leftovers for lunch the next day.

BAKED GREEK SALMON
over ASPARAGUS & RED PEPPERS

SERVES: 4 | **PREP TIME:** 15 minutes | **COOK TIME:** 20 minutes

 DAIRY FREE KETO WHOLE 30 NO ADDED SUGAR

Some nights you have all the time in the world to prepare a delicious home-cooked meal, but most nights you hope to have dinner ready as quickly as possible, and that's when this recipe for Baked Greek Salmon over Asparagus & Red Peppers comes to the rescue. The Greek Vinaigrette provides all the necessary flavor in this one-pan entrée, allowing you more time to sit down and savor a satisfying home-cooked meal.

- 4 wild-caught salmon fillets (skins removed is optional)
- 1 pound (455 g) asparagus spears, tough ends removed
- 2 red bell peppers, thinly sliced and seeds removed
- 1 lemon, thinly sliced and seeds removed

- 6 tablespoons (90 ml) Greek Vinaigrette (page 17)
- 1 teaspoon (5 ml) sea salt
- A dash of white pepper
- ¼ cup (60 ml) fresh parsley, minced
- 1 tablespoon (15 ml) fresh chives, minced

PREHEAT oven to 400° F (200° C).

REMOVE the tough ends from the asparagus by holding each of the spears and gently snapping in two; they will naturally break off 2 to 3 inches from the bottom. Discard ends.

ARRANGE asparagus on a baking tray lined with parchment paper.

THINLY slice red bell peppers and add to the layer of asparagus spears so that both are arranged in the same direction.

DRIZZLE 2 tablespoons (30 ml) of Greek Vinaigrette on the veggies and toss with tongs until veggies are evenly coated.

WASH and pat dry salmon fillets. Coat fillets with 1 tablespoon (15 ml) of Greek Vinaigrette and place on top of the asparagus and peppers.

SPRINKLE salmon and veggies with sea salt and a dash of white pepper, and cover each fillet with thin slices of lemon.

BAKE in the oven for 15 to 20 minutes, or until salmon fillet centers are firm to touch.

REMOVE from the oven and serve with fresh parsley and fresh chives. Enjoy this flavorful Greek salmon and veggie dish as often as possible!

MACRONUTRIENTS: 1 SALMON FILLET PER SERVING | CALORIES: 564 | FAT: 135 G | CARB: 10 G | PROTEIN: 69 G

"Want a game-changing tip? Start thinking about breakfast in different terms by changing the name from 'Breakfast' to 'Meal 1.' That brings about an entirely new perspective, where it's no longer a traditional dish consumed in the morning (like eggs), but just another meal in your three-meals-a-day template. Isn't that freeing? This salmon dish is the perfect light breakfast, designed to boost your brain power and provide long-lasting energy without that annoying 11 AM slump. And if you really wanted to, you could totally put an egg on it. In fact, I've determined you can actually put a fried egg on anything. Trust me. It's science."

—Melissa Hartwig

PISTACHIO-CRUSTED CHICKEN
with SPICY AIOLI

 DAIRY FREE    NO ADDED SUGAR

I have no doubt this recipe will become a favorite! I have taken the classic schnitzel and, to make it anti-inflammatory, reinvented it without using any grain- or dairy-based products. You could swap the chicken for chicken livers or hearts, some wild-caught seafood, or pretty much any other animal protein. Serve with a large salad or cooked vegetables and, of course, some fermented veggies on the side. You can even wrap up the chicken in lettuce or cabbage leaves, and slather it with a flavored mayonnaise or aioli.

2 pounds (900 g) chicken breast fillets

1 cup (250 ml) pistachios

1 cup (250 ml) almond meal

2 tablespoons (30 ml) flat-leaf parsley leaves, finely chopped

1 ½ teaspoons (7.5 ml) chili flakes (optional)

1 teaspoon (5 ml) garlic powder

1 teaspoon (5 ml) onion powder

Sea salt and freshly ground black pepper

2 eggs

2 tablespoons (30 ml) coconut cream or almond milk

⅔ cup (150 ml) tapioca flour

⅔ cup (150 ml) Aioli (page 43)

½ teaspoon (2.5 ml) chipotle chili powder, or to taste

½ teaspoon (2.5 ml) preserved lemon zest, finely chopped

Avocado Oil, for frying

Lemon halves, for garnish

TO make the Spicy Aioli, mix together the aioli, chipotle powder, and preserved lemon zest. Set aside until needed.

BLITZ the pistachios to a fine crumb in a food processor. Transfer to a shallow bowl, add the almond meal, parsley, chili flakes (if using), garlic powder, onion powder, and a pinch each of salt and pepper, and mix well.

PLACE the eggs and coconut cream (or almond milk) in a shallow bowl and whisk well. Place the tapioca flour in another shallow bowl.

CUT the chicken breasts lengthwise into 1-inch (2.5-cm) strips, and pat dry with a paper towel. One by one, dredge the chicken strips in the tapioca flour. Shake off any excess flour, dip in the egg mixture, and then coat in the nut crumb mixture, being sure to cover the entire chicken strip thoroughly. If there are areas that are not entirely coated, simply dab a little more egg mixture onto the dry spot and coat again with the nut crumbs.

HEAT the oil in a large frying pan over medium-high heat. Add the crumbed chicken strips, in batches, and cook for 2 ½ to 3 minutes on each side until golden brown and cooked through. Drain on a paper towel. Allow to cool slightly before serving. Season with salt, if needed.

SERVE the Pistachio-Crusted Chicken with the Spicy Aioli and some lemon halves on the side.

MACRONUTRIENTS: 1 CUP PER SERVING | CALORIES: 936 | FAT: 57 G | CARB: 35 G | PROTEIN: 72 G

"Moderation is okay, until it isn't. If you value your health (both physical and mental), then you will make the right choices that reinforce that value. If you don't value your health, then you will think that a little bit of this or that is okay...until it isn't."

—Pete Evans

MARINATED FILET MIGNONS

SERVES: 2 | PREP TIME: 1 hour 30 minutes | COOK TIME: 10 minutes

 DAIRY FREE   KETO   WHOLE 30   NO ADDED SUGAR

The filet is from the most tender, smallest, and desirable end of the tenderloin. (It's not called "tender"-loin for nothing!) It's also the most expensive. Preparing filet mignons at home will save you 2 to 5 times the money for the same cut at a restaurant. Ah ha, got your attention now!

- 2 half-pound (225 g) filets
- 3 tablespoons (45 ml) Greek Vinaigrette (page 17)
- 2 tablespoons (30 ml) garlic powder
- 1 tablespoon (15 ml) onion powder
- 2 tablespoons (30 ml) coarse-cracked pepper
- Sea salt and coarse-ground black pepper to taste

DRY your filets and pierce them with a fork on all sides.

MIX the Greek Vinaigrette, garlic powder, onion powder, and pepper in a bowl using a wire whisk, and then pour into a flat square dish.

MARINATE the filets in this mixture in the refrigerator for 1 hour, flipping once halfway through.

REMOVE filets from the refrigerator and let sit to room temperature, about 20 to 30 minutes, to ensure even cooking.

PREHEAT your grill to 500° F (260° C) and grease the grill racks with avocado oil.

GRILL for about 4 minutes on each side.

USE a meat thermometer to test the internal temperature. If you prefer your steak rare, 120° to 125° F (45° to 50° C), the filets will be ready at this point and you may remove them from the heat. If you're like me, I prefer to gently cook the sides a bit more. Reduce the heat and lightly brown the sides of the filets. For medium rare, cook until the internal temperature reads 130° to 135° F (55° to 60° C), 140° to 145° F (60° to 65° C) for medium, 150° to 155° F (65° to 70° C) for medium-well, and 160° F and above (70° C and above) for well done.

PLACE the filets on plates or a platter and cover with foil. Let rest for 4 minutes.

SERVE with salt and pepper.

MACRONUTRIENTS: 1 FILET PER SERVING | CALORIES: 739 | FAT: 162 G | CARB: 12 G | PROTEIN: 46 G

HONEY MUSTARD CHICKEN
and SWEET POTATO

SERVES: 4 to 5 | **PREP TIME:** 24 hours 30 minutes | **COOK TIME:** 45 minutes

 DAIRY FREE  NO ADDED SUGAR

I can't remember the last time I made something THIS epic. I had a feeling we had a rockstar on our hands when this one-pot meal was baking and the smell was wafting through the house, but it wasn't until my kids took a bite that I was sure. Every kid devoured it. And then asked for seconds. If the kids are that wild about a recipe, then you know it's outstanding. I am SO excited for you to make this recipe. SO. EXCITED.

- 2 pounds (900 g) boneless skinless chicken breast, cut into pieces
- 1 yellow onion, chopped
- 2 cloves garlic, minced
- 1 heaping teaspoon (5 ml) fresh ginger, minced
- 1 ½ teaspoons (7.5 ml) mixed salt (such as Herbamare®), use divided
- 1 cup (6 oz) (170 g) unsulfured dried apricots, halved

- ½ cup (125 ml) Honey Mustard Vinaigrette (page 19)
- ½ cup (125 ml) orange juice
- 1 red bell pepper, chopped
- 4 sweet potatoes, peeled and chopped
- Fresh thyme to garnish (optional)

ADD the chicken breast, yellow onion, minced garlic, and ginger, ½ teaspoon (2.5 ml) mixed salt, and dried apricots to a 9x13-inch (33x23x5-cm) baking dish.

POUR the Honey Mustard Vinaigrette and orange juice over the top, and use a spatula to toss until well combined. Put the lid on and marinate in the fridge for 24 hours.

SET the oven for 350° F (180° C). Toss the red bell pepper, sweet potatoes, and remaining 1 teaspoon of mixed salt in a mixing bowl, and then add ingredients to the marinated chicken mixture. Use a spatula to toss all ingredients until well combined.

BAKE for 45 minutes. Remove from the oven. Optional: drizzle the top with avocado oil and garnish with fresh thyme.

MACRONUTRIENTS: 1 ¼ CUPS PER SERVING | CALORIES: 699 | FAT: 24 G | CARB: 55 G | PROTEIN: 64 G

BASIL PORK BURGERS with MUSHROOMS and BASIL GARLIC MAYO

SERVES: 8 TO 10 | PREP TIME: 35 minutes | COOK TIME: 10 minutes

 DAIRY FREE · KETO · WHOLE 30 · NO ADDED SUGAR

These burgers are so good you'll need to be prepared for total food nirvana, and the chances of eating more than one burger is incredibly high. Even 4-year-old children will be quiet at the dinner table as these burgers are messily and happily consumed. Consider yourself deliciously forewarned.

2 pounds (900 g) ground pork

½ cup (125 ml) fresh basil leaves, diced

½ teaspoon (2.5 ml) sea salt

2 teaspoons (10 ml) black pepper

6 cups (1 16-ounce package) sliced crimini or white mushrooms

1 yellow onion, diced

¼ cup (60 ml) Avocado Oil

1 cup (250 ml) Classic Mayo (page 13)

2 garlic cloves, minced

⅓ cup (75 ml) basil, finely chopped

TO make the burgers, mix the first four ingredients together and shape into eight to ten even-sized patties. Grill or pan-fry over medium heat. Start out cooking for 4 minutes on one side (or until browned); flip and cook for another 3 to 4 minutes on the other side. If you make your burgers really thick, flip again and repeat the same cook time on both sides.

WITH pork burgers, cook those babies until they are no longer pink in the middle, but watch them carefully because you do not want them to overcook and dry out! For best results, you can check for doneness with a meat thermometer. Internal temp of the burgers should be 160° F (71°C).

WHILE the burgers are cooking, get started on the mushrooms. In a large skillet, pour the avocado oil over medium to medium-high heat. Add the onions and sauté until translucent. Add the mushrooms to the onions and sauté until the mushrooms are tender. Season with a little sea salt and black pepper.

MIX Classic Mayo with the basil and the garlic. Serve the burgers on a large piece of Romaine lettuce topped with mushrooms, and add a dollop of basil garlic mayo.

MACRONUTRIENTS: 1 BURGER PER SERVING | CALORIES: 502 | FAT: 46 G | CARB: 3 G | PROTEIN: 8 G

STEAK
with ROMESCO SAUCE

SERVES: 2 | PREP TIME: 10 minutes | COOK TIME: 10 minutes

DAIRY FREE · KETO · WHOLE 30 · NO ADDED SUGAR

Romesco is a Spanish sauce made from tomatoes, red peppers, garlic, and almonds. Nutritious and flavorful, it can be served with any type of meat or seafood. It also tastes great with eggs, so don't hesitate to scramble up a few to serve alongside the steak.

½ pound (225 g) skirt steak	1 roasted red pepper
1 cup (250 ml) cherry tomatoes	¼ cup (60 ml) Avocado Oil
¼ cup (60 ml) almonds, whole or sliced	1 tablespoon (15 ml) sherry vinegar
2 garlic cloves	¼ teaspoon (1.25 ml) red pepper flakes

ROASTED red peppers are sold in grocery stores and save time, but you can also roast your own. Simply blacken the red pepper under a broiler or over an open flame, let the pepper cool, then remove the burnt skin under running water.

HEAT a skillet over medium-high heat. Lightly salt and pepper the steak. Place it on one side of the pan, and the tomatoes, almonds, and garlic cloves on the other side.

STIR the tomatoes, almonds, and garlic a few times, so they brown evenly. After 3 minutes, flip the steak. Cook 2 minutes more, and scoop the tomatoes, garlic, and almonds into a food processor or blender. Keep the steak in the pan and continue to cook until done (thinly sliced steak will only need a few minutes more).

ADD the roasted red pepper, avocado oil, sherry vinegar, and red pepper flakes to the food processor or blender, and pulse until smooth.

SERVE the Romesco sauce drizzled over the steak.

MACRONUTRIENTS: 4 OUNCES STEAK PER SERVING | CALORIES: 610 | FAT: 52 G | CARB: 11 G | PROTEIN: 28 G

SLOW COOKER
BUFFALO CHICKEN-STUFFED SWEET POTATO

SERVES: 4 | **PREP TIME:** 30 minutes | **COOK TIME:** 6 hours

 DAIRY FREE WHOLE 30 *option* NO ADDED SUGAR

While this isn't a chicken wing recipe per se, it most definitely will satisfy that ongoing craving for "wing sauce." And even if you're not a Buffalo chicken wing fan (like me), I think you'll be pleasantly surprised by how much you like this recipe. It's gotta be the addition of the sweet potatoes and ranch! Speaking of sweet potatoes, if you'd rather serve the slow cooker Buffalo chicken in a lettuce wrap, paleo tortillas, or on gluten-free bread, by all means, go for it!

½ pound (225 g) boneless, skinless chicken breast

½ pound (225 g) boneless, skinless chicken thighs

⅓ cup (75 ml) hot sauce*

2 tablespoons (30 ml) ghee

1 tablespoon (15 ml) coconut aminos

½ teaspoon (2.5 ml) garlic powder

¼ teaspoon (1.25 ml) cayenne (optional)

4 small baked sweet potatoes

Wild Ranch Dressing (page 21), for topping

PLACE chicken in a slow cooker set on low.

IN a small saucepan on medium-high heat, combine the hot sauce, ghee, coconut aminos, garlic powder, and optional cayenne. Stir together and heat until ghee is melted.

POUR sauce into the slow cooker.

COOK for 4 to 6 hours on low, or until chicken is tender.

REMOVE chicken from the slow cooker and shred with two forks. Return shredded chicken to the slow cooker and toss with sauce.

TURN the slow cooker to warm (or remain on low) until ready to serve.

SERVE chicken in baked sweet potatoes and drizzle with ranch, if desired.

*USE Whole30 Approved hot sauce for a Whole30-approved recipe.

MACRONUTRIENTS: 1 POTATO PER SERVING | CALORIES: 461 | FAT: 19 G | CARB: 39 G | PROTEIN: 34 G

HONEY MUSTARD SALMON

SERVES: 1 | **PREP TIME:** 25 minutes | **COOK TIME:** 18 minutes

 DAIRY FREE   KETO   NO ADDED SUGAR

A simple and delicious way to dress up salmon fillets with minimal ingredients and effort! Pairs beautifully with a citrus salad or cauliflower rice.

1 salmon fillet

1 cup (250 ml) Honey Mustard Vinaigrette (page 19)

1 lemon, sliced

Salt and pepper to taste

PLACE the salmon fillet and Honey Mustard Vinaigrette in a large ziplock bag. Using your hands, lightly incorporate the vinaigrette into the salmon. Marinate the salmon fillet for 20 minutes.

REMOVE salmon and place on lined baking sheet, skin side down.

PLACE lemon slices on the salmon. Sprinkle with salt and pepper.

COOK salmon at 400° F (200° C) for 18 minutes, or until salmon flakes with a fork.

MACRONUTRIENTS: 1 SALMON FILLET PER SERVING | CALORIES: 509 | FAT: 23 G | CARB: 7 G | PROTEIN: 66 G

BISON CHILI

SERVES: 3 to 4 | PREP TIME: 15 minutes | COOK TIME: 45 minutes

 DAIRY FREE   KETO   WHOLE 30 *option*   NO ADDED SUGAR

Here I am, getting you to eat your offal. This recipe sneaks it in undercover and is so delicious, you'll forget you ever disliked organ meat. The ingredient list may seem like a lot, but the recipe itself is actually very easy to make. If you don't like a component, then remove it. If you want to add your own favorites or veggies, do it. Be mindful that if you add veggies, you'll want to up the spices a touch to ensure maximum flavor.

2 tablespoons (30 ml) Avocado Oil

½ yellow onion, chopped

1 large heirloom tomato, diced

1 tablespoon (15 ml) espresso, finely ground

1 garlic clove, chopped

1 pound (455 g) ground bison blend (heart, liver, meat)

2 tablespoons (30 ml) chili powder

1 tablespoon (15 ml) cumin

½ tablespoon (7.5 ml) garlic powder

1 teaspoon (5 ml) onion powder

¼ teaspoon (1.25 ml) cayenne

1 teaspoon (5 ml) salt

¾ cup (175 ml) tomato paste

1 tablespoon (15 ml) coconut teriyaki sauce*

2 tablespoons (30 ml) Greek Vinaigrette (page 17)

Water, as needed

IN a large pot, add avocado oil, and begin sautéing onions. Continue cooking until they are quite dark (almost black on pieces). Then mix in diced tomatoes, espresso grounds and garlic.

ADD the bison blend, mashing it into the pan with a large fork or potato masher.

THEN, add all the spices and more cooking fat, if necessary. Continue mashing the meat blend, until separated into a fine texture.

I like to keep it slightly undercooked while adding the tomato concentrate, Greek Vinaigrette, and coconut teriyaki sauce. Continue mashing.

ADD a ½ cup (125 ml) of water at a time, until you get the consistency you desire. Let it simmer for 15 to 20 minutes over medium heat.

ADD salt and other preferred seasonings to taste. (I like a combination of tangy, sweet, and spicy all at once.)

TURN down the heat, let it thicken up, and BOOM—you've got yourself a seriously power-packed chili dish that'll last you a few days.

*OMIT coconut teriyaki sauce for a Whole30-approved recipe.

MACRONUTRIENTS: 1 CUP PER SERVING | CALORIES: 535 | FAT: 86 G | CARB: 12 G | PROTEIN: 22 G

"The way you eat, the way you play, the way you live…
it's all preparation for everything *right* in your life."

—Mary Shenouda, The Paleo Chef

BEEF SLIDERS
with CHIPOTLE LIME MAYO

SERVES: 5 | PREP TIME: 25 minutes | COOK TIME: 15 minutes

 DAIRY FREE   KETO   *option*    NO ADDED SUGAR

These bunless beef sliders are a healthy, flavorful grilled dinner dream come true! I place perfectly cooked beef sliders on a pile of fresh butter lettuce, tomato, purple onion, and a couple of avocado slices. The whole meal comes together with delicious Chipotle Lime Mayo! Served alongside some tiny pickles, this is one easy, tasty, and filling dinner.

1 ¼ pounds (570 g) ground beef

½ teaspoon (2.5 ml) fine sea salt

¼ teaspoon (1.25 ml) cracked
   black pepper

1 tablespoon (15 ml) Avocado Oil

5 to 10 pieces butter lettuce

2 medium-sized tomatoes,
   sliced ½ inch thick (13 mm)

¼ purple onion, thinly sliced

½ avocado, thinly sliced

¼ cup (60 ml) Chipotle Lime Mayo*
   (page 15)

2 tablespoons (30 ml) fresh lime juice

FORM ground beef into 10 slider patties, approximately 2 ounces each.

PREHEAT the grill, stovetop grill, or oiled frying pan over high heat. Season both sides of the patties with the salt and pepper. Once the grill is at temperature, sear the patties for about 3 minutes on each side, or until they develop char marks. Once finished cooking (they cook fast!), transfer to a plate to rest.

WHISK Chipotle Lime Mayo and lime juice together until smooth, and set aside until assembly.

TO assemble, lay the lettuce down first, followed by the tomato slices, onion, and avocado. Top with 2 burger patties and drizzle with Chipotle Lime Mayo.

*USE Primal Kitchen brand Chipotle Lime Mayo for a Whole30-approved recipe.

MACRONUTRIENTS: 2 SLIDERS PER SERVING | CALORIES: 446 | FAT: 36 G | CARB: 9 G | PROTEIN: 22 G

Alanna Figueira, Planks, Love & Guacamole

CHICKEN POT PIE SOUP
with DROP BISCUITS

SERVES: 6 | PREP TIME: 45 minutes | COOK TIME: 30 minutes

 DAIRY FREE

You will love this creamy, dreamy, comforting soup, especially when the weather is crisp! This classic remake is so rich and delicious, with hints of thyme and nutmeg, that the whole family can enjoy it, without any reactions to the traditionally-used heavy cream and cornstarch. This Chicken Pot Pie Soup is topped with a biscuit pillow that is crispy on the outside, fluffy on the inside, perfect for soaking up that wonderfully creamy soup.

¼ cup (60 ml) Avocado Oil

¾ cup (175 ml) onion, chopped

¾ cup (175 ml) celery, chopped

2 cups (450 g) frozen veggies of choice, chopped

1 ½ teaspoons (7.5 ml) dried thyme

1 ½ teaspoons (7.5 ml) poultry seasoning

1 ¼ teaspoons (6.25 ml) salt

1 teaspoon (5 ml) black pepper

½ teaspoon (2.5 ml) nutmeg

3 tablespoons (45 ml) arrowroot flour

2 cups (500 ml) rotisserie chicken

3 ½ cups (875 ml) chicken broth

⅓ cup (75 ml) coconut cream

¼ cup (60 ml) Classic Mayo (page 13)

⅓ cup (75 ml) cassava flour

⅓ cup (75 ml) almond flour

2 tablespoons (30 ml) coconut flour

1 tablespoon (15 ml) baking powder

½ teaspoon (2.5 ml) salt

1 egg

2 tablespoons (30 ml) Avocado Oil

½ cup coconut (125 ml) milk

1 tablespoon (15 ml) honey

TO pull the meat from the chicken, first, let the chicken cool enough to handle, if it's fresh from the store. Start by removing and discarding the skin. Next, remove the legs and wings and pull off the meat with a fork or your fingers. Dice the meat into cubes, and then place it in a large bowl. Then, pull or cut off the breast meat and dice. Once all meat is removed and diced, add it to the bowl. A 2-pound (900 g) chicken will yield approximately 2 to 3 cups (250 g to 375 g) of diced meat.

IN a medium, heavy-bottomed soup pot, pour in avocado oil. Add chopped celery, onions, frozen veggies, thyme, poultry seasoning, salt, pepper, and nutmeg. Cook until veggies are tender. Sprinkle in arrowroot, mixing well with the veggies. When everything is combined, mix in the chicken.

ADD broth. Simmer on medium low for a few minutes. Lastly, mix in the coconut cream and mayo, still over medium-low heat, and mix to combine.

SET aside.

TO make drop biscuits: Preheat oven to 425° F (230° C) and line a cookie sheet with parchment paper.

ADD cassava flour, almond flour, coconut flour, baking powder, and salt to a large mixing bowl, and mix to combine.

IN a separate bowl, whisk egg, avocado oil, coconut milk, and honey to combine.

ADD the wet to the dry. Mix to combine.

IF sheet baking the biscuits, drop blobs of batter onto a parchment-lined cookie sheet.

IF making biscuits in the soup, arrange six ramekins on a baking tray and ladle soup into them, filling about ¾ of the way. Drop about three blobs of batter on each ramekin top.

BAKE 8 to 10 minutes for sheet-pan drop biscuits.

BAKE less for soup drop biscuits. Cooking time will vary based on how big the biscuits are on top of soups, so check on them from 5 minutes on.

MACRONUTRIENTS: ¾ CUP PER SERVING | CALORIES:531 | FAT: 41 G | CARB: 23 G | PROTEIN: 20 G

"Neither of my kids tolerate dairy, and one of my greatest challenges
is re-creating creamy comfort dishes. I find mayo to be a lifesaver;
it gives creaminess to sauces, dressings, and casseroles.
The best part is that a little bit goes a long way."

—Alanna Figueira, Planks, Love & Guacamole

MEDITERRANEAN MARINATED ROAST

SERVES: 4 | **PREP TIME:** 4 hours 20 minutes | **COOK TIME:** 2 hours 40 minutes

 DAIRY FREE   KETO   WHOLE 30   NO ADDED SUGAR

If you think Chuck Roast is boring, think again! Marinated in flavorful Greek Vinaigrette, slow roasted, and basted with red wine, this chuck is simple to make, but turns out elegant and tender.

2 pounds (900 g) chuck roast

1 white onion, sliced

½ cup (125 ml) Greek Vinaigrette (page 17)

¼ cup (60 ml) red wine*

¼ cup (60 ml) bone broth*

1 teaspoon (5 ml) salt

1 teaspoon (5 ml) black pepper

2 tablespoons (30 ml) sugar-free bacon fat or Avocado Oil

PLACE chuck roast in a large bowl or container. Add salt and pepper to Greek Vinaigrette, mix to combine, and then pour over the roast, massaging the marinade into the meat. Smother with onion slices.

COVER and set in fridge to marinate for at least 4 hours.

SET oven to 225 F (107°C). When ready to cook, heat a large cast iron skillet over high heat and add fat or oil to the skillet. Sear chuck roast on all sides until browned, about 1 minute per side. Arrange onions from marinade on top of the roast, as well as any leftover marinade. Place in the oven to slow cook at 225° F (107°C).

MIX wine and bone broth in a measuring cup.

AFTER an hour in the oven, pour half of the wine/broth mix over the roast. Slow roast for another hour, and then pour the remaining wine/broth mixture over the roast. Roast for 30 more minutes. Internal temperature should be around 140° to 145° F (160° C) when done.

LET the roast rest a few minutes before slicing and serving.

*OMIT red wine and use an additional ¼ cup of Whole30 Approved bone broth (½ cup total) for a Whole30-approved recipe.

MACRONUTRIENTS: 8 OUNCES PER SERVING | CALORIES: 648 | FAT: 51 G | CARB: 3 G | PROTEIN: 59 G

CHIPOTLE CHICKEN ENCHILADAS

SERVES: 4 | PREP TIME: 30 minutes | COOK TIME: 25 minutes

 DAIRY FREE *option*    NO ADDED SUGAR

Chipotle Chicken Enchiladas have become a weekly staple in our house. They're rich, flavorful, and perfect for a quick and easy weeknight meal!

2 pounds (900 g) rotisserie chicken

1 can (127 g) diced green chilies

½ cup (125 ml) Chipotle Lime Mayo (page 15)

½ teaspoon (2.5 ml) salt

½ teaspoon (2.5 ml) pepper

¼ cup (60 ml) diced onion

1 ½ tablespoons (22.5 ml) Avocado Oil, divided

8 Cassava Flour Tortillas (page 135)

3 ½ cups (875 ml) Enchilada Sauce (page 47)

1 cup (250 ml) shredded cheese*

1 avocado, pitted

½ cup (125 ml) cilantro, chopped

1 green onion, chopped

1 jalapeño (optional)

PREHEAT oven to 350° F (180°C).

TO pull the meat from the chicken, first, let the chicken cool enough to handle, if it's fresh from the store. Remove the skin. You can chop the skin up and use it for the recipe, if you'd like, or you can discard it. Next, remove the legs and wings and pull the meat off with a fork or your fingers. Using two forks, shred the meat on a cutting board, and then add shredded meat to a large bowl. Then, pull or cut off the breast meat and shred with your forks. Once all meat is removed and shredded, add it to the bowl. A 2-pound (900 g) chicken will yield approximately 2 to 3 cups (250 g to 375 g) of shredded meat.

IN a large saucepan at medium heat, add in 1 tablespoon (15 ml) of avocado oil along with chopped onion, and cook for 3 minutes.

ADD chilies, shredded chicken, salt, pepper, and mayo to the pan and mix well. Once combined, remove from heat and set aside.

OIL the bottom of a 9x13 pan (33x23x5 cm), with ½ tablespoon (22.5 ml) of avocado oil. Then add ¼-cup (60 ml) Enchilada Sauce, spreading evenly across the bottom of the pan.

IF Cassava Flour Tortillas aren't freshly made, lay them flat on a cookie sheet and put in the oven for 1 to 1 ½ minutes to soften.

CAREFULLY remove the tortillas and fill each tortilla with chicken mixture. Roll and lay into the pan.

ONCE all tortillas are filled and placed in the pan, top with the remaining Enchilada Sauce.

TOP with shredded cheese and bake for 20 minutes.

SERVE with jalapeño slices, avocado, cilantro, and green onion.

EAT immediately or store in an airtight container in the fridge.

*OMIT cheese for a dairy-free recipe.

"Living a balanced life is the key to your well-being. Find joy in the balance.
Eat well, breathe deeply, laugh out loud, and think positively.
Nourish your body and mind by doing something
you love every day, and celebrate yourself
through every season of life."

—Amy Sheree

LAMB BURGERS
with PISTACHIO PESTO

SERVES: 4 | **PREP TIME:** 20 minutes | **COOK TIME:** 12 minutes

 DAIRY FREE KETO WHOLE 30  NO ADDED SUGAR

Richer than your average burger, this dish is a nice change from the usual beef burger with mustard and ketchup. The pistachio pesto has such a thick texture you won't even miss the cheese.

1 ½ pounds (675 g) ground lamb

1 teaspoon (5 ml) cumin

¼ teaspoon (1.25 ml) cinnamon

¼ teaspoon (1.25 ml) allspice

½ teaspoon (2.5 ml) salt

¼ teaspoon (1.25 ml) black pepper

¼ cup (60 ml) mint leaves, finely chopped

¼ cup (60 ml) parsley, chopped

1 garlic clove

1 cup (250 ml) pistachios

½ cup (125 ml) Avocado Oil

1 teaspoon (5 ml) lemon juice, or more to taste

¼ cup (60 ml) mint leaves, loosely packed

A pinch of sea salt

MIX together the ground lamb, spices, chopped mint, and parsley. Form four patties and pan-fry or grill them, about 4 to 6 minutes per side.

WHILE the burgers are cooking, blend together garlic, pistachios, avocado oil, lemon juice, whole mint leaves, and salt in a food processor.

SERVE burgers with pesto drizzled on top.

MACRONUTRIENTS: 1 BURGER PER SERVING | CALORIES: 813 | FAT: 74 G | CARB: 6 G | PROTEIN: 32 G

CREAMY SPICED
TURMERIC CHICKEN THIGHS

SERVES: 4 to 6 │ **PREP TIME:** 15 minutes │ **COOK TIME:** 45 minutes

 DAIRY FREE   KETO   WHOLE 30 *option*   NO ADDED SUGAR

Roasting bone-in chicken thighs is one of the many pleasures the primal lifestyle has to offer. Crispy skin, melt-in-your-mouth chicken...does it get any better? It certainly does with this unique blend of spicy Chipotle Lime Mayo, turmeric, lemon juice, herbs, and black pepper! Rich in anti-inflammatory curcumin, this dish helps your body heal while pleasing your palate. It is simple to prepare, yet yields complex flavors sure to tempt even those who've always thought they did not enjoy mayonnaise. Try it for yourself and discover how rewarding roasting chicken really is.

6 organic bone-in chicken thighs

2 tablespoons (30 ml) ghee

½ cup (125 ml) Chipotle Lime Mayo*
(page 15)

1 teaspoon (5 ml) sea salt

1 teaspoon (5 ml) ground turmeric

1 teaspoon (5 ml) dried
Herbes de Provence

1 teaspoon (5 ml) dried onion powder

½ teaspoon (2.5 ml) dried garlic powder

¼ teaspoon (1.25 ml) ground black pepper

1 tablespoon (15 ml) fresh lemon juice

Fresh parsley, for garnish

Fresh lemon wedges, for garnish

PREHEAT oven to 350° F (180° C).

RINSE chicken thighs and pat dry with a paper towel. Rub chicken with ghee and arrange on a baking tray lined with parchment paper, or in a cast iron skillet.

TO make the Spiced Turmeric Herb Sauce, add Chipotle Lime Mayo, salt, turmeric, Herbes de Provence, onion powder, garlic powder, pepper, and lemon juice to a medium-size mixing bowl, and whisk until well combined. The turmeric will make the sauce a rich golden color (be careful not to get the sauce on your clothing, because turmeric does stain!).

USING a baker's spatula, coat each chicken thigh with the Spiced Turmeric Herb Sauce.

PLACE chicken in the oven and roast uncovered for 40 minutes. After 40 minutes, turn on your broiler to high and cook for 5 more minutes. The broiler will give your chicken a delicious crispy finish, while the sauce traps the chicken's juices, ensuring a super satisfying meal.

SERVE chicken thighs on a platter and garnish with freshly minced parsley and lemon wedges.

*USE Primal Kitchen brand Chipotle Lime Mayo for a Whole30-approved recipe.

"Remember, cooking is fun! The kitchen is where you feel accomplished, creative, and proud of the fact that you took these ingredients and made this meal and nourished your loved ones. You might mess some meals up. Rarely will they be inedible. Your meals may turn out ugly, but taste delicious. This is winning in my book. Your kitchen may look like a bomb went off after making something relatively simple. Don't stress, because it gets easier. Remember any new skill requires practice and dedication, and the best part about practicing this skill is that you get to eat the end results!"

—Melissa Hartwig

HAZELNUT-CRUSTED HALIBUT

SERVES: 2 | **PREP TIME:** 15 minutes | **COOK TIME:** 15 minutes

 DAIRY FREE · KETO · WHOLE 30 · NO ADDED SUGAR

Most Americans are getting too much omega-6 fatty acid from the wrong sources and not enough omega-3 fatty acid from any source in their diet. This recipe is a great way to correct that balance with a healthier source of omega-6 from avocado mayo, and one of the best sources of omega-3 from halibut. Haven't tried baking fish with mayo? You're going to love this chef's secret!

2 8-ounce (225 g) halibut fillets

1 tablespoons (15 ml) Avocado Oil

1 cup (250 ml) Classic Mayo (page 13)

1 ½ cups (375 ml) hazelnuts,
    very finely chopped

1 lemon, juiced

Salt and white pepper to taste

2 tablespoons (30 ml) fresh chives, chopped

PREHEAT oven to 375° F (190° C).

GREASE the baking dish with Avocado Oil.

SALT and pepper the fillets and thoroughly coat with Classic Mayo.

ROLL the fillets in the hazelnuts and place in a baking dish.

BAKE for 15 minutes, or until the fish flakes easily with a fork.

KEEP a close eye while baking, as the hazelnuts can burn easily. If in doubt, drop the oven temperature to 350° F (180° C). Most slow baking is done at this temperature.

SEPARATE the fillets onto two plates, squeeze the lemon juice over them, and garnish with chives.

MACRONUTRIENTS: 1 HALIBUT FILLET PER SERVING | CALORIES: 1,780 | FAT: 175 G | CARB: 15 G | PROTEIN: 46 G

CHICKEN CAESAR BURGERS

SERVES: 4 | **PREP TIME:** 20 minutes | **COOK TIME:** 10 minutes

DAIRY FREE *option*   KETO   WHOLE 30 *option*   NO ADDED SUGAR

We use mayo to whip up a creamy Caesar dressing for use on some chicken burgers. It's our play on deconstructing a Caesar salad and turning it into a burger. The chicken burgers themselves have a unique flavor thanks to the capers and coconut aminos, and with the Caesar dressing on top, it makes the whole thing truly decadent.

1 pound (455 g) ground chicken

2 tablespoons (30 ml) onion, minced

½ tablespoon (7.5 ml) capers, chopped

½ tablespoon (7.5 ml) fresh parsley, minced

1 clove garlic, minced

½ tablespoon (7.5 ml) coconut aminos

Sea salt and freshly ground black pepper to taste

Avocado Oil for cooking

4 tablespoons (60 ml) Caesar Dressing (page 25)

Romaine lettuce leaves

Tomato, thinly sliced

Red onion, thinly sliced

GENTLY mix chicken, onion, capers, parsley, garlic, coconut aminos, salt, and pepper in a bowl. Then form four equally sized patties.

HEAT a grill pan or skillet with a small amount of avocado oil over medium-high heat.

WHEN hot, add the chicken patties and cook for 4 to 5 minutes on each side, or until the center reaches 165° F (74° C) and the juices run clear.

SERVE the burgers on a bed of romaine topped with Caesar Dressing, tomato slices, or onion, if you'd like.

*OMIT Parmigiano-Reggiano cheese when preparing the Caesar Dressing for a dairy-free and Whole30-approved recipe.

MACRONUTRIENTS: 1 BURGER PER SERVING | CALORIES: 369 | FAT: 25 G | CARB: 3 G | PROTEIN: 32 G

HONEY MUSTARD VINAIGRETTE SHORT RIBS and RADICCHIO SALAD

SERVES: 4 | **PREP TIME:** 2 hours 15 minutes | **COOK TIME:** 15 minutes

DAIRY FREE   NO ADDED SUGAR

Honey Mustard Vinaigrette serves double-duty here as a marinade for meat and a dressing for salads. The vinaigrette does all the work, while you sit back and relax. There's no chopping or stirring needed to put this four-ingredient meal together. And your kitchen will stay so clean, it won't even look like you've made dinner.

1 ½ pounds (675 g) boneless short ribs

½ cup (125 ml) plus ¼ cup (60 ml) Honey Mustard Vinaigrette (page 19), divided

1 head radicchio

4 large handfuls arugula

Avocado Oil, for grilling

IN a large sealable plastic bag, combine the short ribs with a ½ cup (120 ml) of Honey Mustard Vinaigrette. Toss and turn the bag to make sure all the meat is coated in vinaigrette. Marinate 2 hours in the refrigerator.

REMOVE the ribs from the marinade, and season lightly with salt.

PREPARE a grill for medium-high heat; lightly oil the grate with avocado oil.

GRILL short ribs, turning as needed until lightly charred on all sides, 8 to 12 minutes total.

LET the ribs rest 10 minutes, and then slice against the grain.

WHILE the ribs are resting, cut the radicchio into fourths, leaving the leaves attached at the bottom core. Brush the wedges lightly with avocado oil. Grill the radicchio wedges 1 to 2 minutes on each side, until charred. Remove from the grill, trim off the bottom core, and thinly slice the leaves.

IN a large bowl, toss the radicchio and arugula with a ¼ cup (60 ml) of Honey Mustard Vinaigrette.

SERVE the sliced short ribs over the radicchio and arugula salad.

MACRONUTRIENTS: 6 OUNCES PER SERVING | CALORIES: 848 | FAT: 76 G | CARB: 2 G | PROTEIN: 37 G

DESSERTS

Don't worry, I haven't gone soft, but I do realize that life calls for a bit of indulgence every once in awhile. With all the delectable options out there, why settle for the typical processed and sugar-laden desserts? If you're going to indulge, I suggest you make it something tasty and reasonably good for you. The idea here is to create treats with the least amount of processing and the highest nutritional benefits.

BERRY CRUMBLE

SERVES: 2 | PREP TIME: 15 minutes | COOK TIME: 40 minutes

 DAIRY FREE

Before you scoff at the mayo in this recipe, remember that mayonnaise is really just oil and eggs—classic ingredients in any baked good. Pair it with fresh berries and a little spice, and you've got yourself the perfect antioxidant-rich, healthy-fat treat!

- 1 ⅓ cup (225 g) fresh berries
- 1 cup (250 ml) coconut flour
- ⅓ cup (75 ml) coconut sugar

- ½ teaspoon (2.5 ml) cinnamon
- 2 tablespoons (30 ml) Classic Mayo (page 13)

PREHEAT oven to 350° F (175° C). Place ⅔ cup (100 g) berries into two 6-ounce (170 g) ramekins.

IN a medium bowl, stir together the flour, sugar, and cinnamon. Stir in the mayonnaise until the mixture resembles coarse crumbs. Fork apart if necessary.

SPRINKLE over the top of the berries.

BAKE for 35 to 40 minutes in the preheated oven, until the top is lightly browned.

MACRONUTRIENTS: 1 6-OUNCE RAMEKIN PER SERVING | CALORIES: 486 | FAT: 19 G | CARB: 72 G | PROTEIN: 9 G

DOUBLE CHOCOLATE CHUNK COOKIES

SERVES: 15 | **PREP TIME:** 15 minutes | **COOK TIME:** 14 minutes

DAIRY FREE
option

Chocolate Coconut Primal Fuel and large chunks of dark chocolate take these cookies to the next level. They are crispy on the outside and fluffy and chewy on the inside. Added bonus: these cookies are chock-full of protein and healthy fats to keep you powered throughout the day!

1 ¾ cups (425 ml) blanched almond flour

3 scoops (63 g) Chocolate Coconut Primal Fuel,* or protein powder of choice

¼ teaspoon (1.25 ml) baking soda

⅓ cup ghee (75 ml), melted

¼ cup honey (60 ml) or pure maple syrup

2 tablespoons (30 ml) almond milk

⅓ cup (75 ml) chopped dark chocolate*

½ teaspoon (2.5 ml) coarse sea salt

PREHEAT oven to 350° F (180°C) and line a cookie sheet with parchment paper.

IN a medium bowl, whisk together the almond flour, protein powder, and baking soda.

IN a small bowl, whisk together the ghee, honey, and almond milk.

STIR the wet ingredients into the dry and mix until dough forms. Stir in the chocolate chunks.

USING a cookie scoop or a heaping tablespoon, scoop the cookie dough onto the baking sheet. Space the balls at least 1 ½ inches (3.8 cm) apart. Flatten them down halfway with the palm of your hand.

SPRINKLE the cookies with the coarse sea salt.

BAKE the cookies for 12 to 14 minutes, then let them cool for about 5 minutes.

STORE leftover cookies in an airtight container at room temperature.

*USE your favorite dairy-free protein powder and dark chocolate for a dairy-free recipe

MACRONUTRIENTS: 1 COOKIE PER SERVING | CALORIES: 169 | FAT: 14 G | CARB: 11 G | PROTEIN: 5 G

COCONUT CASHEW BONBONS

SERVES: 6 | PREP TIME: 40 minutes

 VEGAN *option*    DAIRY FREE

What could be more delicious than a Primal Kitchen Coconut Cashew Bar? A Coconut Cashew Bonbon, of course! Get creative with this recipe and use any variety of Primal Kitchen collagen bars or your favorite protein bar—or combine two flavors together for the ultimate custom treat.

1 Primal Kitchen Coconut Cashew Bar* (48 g), or your favorite collagen/protein bar

2 tablespoons (30 ml) unsweetened cocoa

¼ cup (60 ml) unsweetened almond butter

2 ⅓ tablespoons (35 ml) maple syrup

1 tablespoon (15 ml) coconut oil

¹⁄₁₆ teaspoon (0.31 ml) Himalayan sea salt

Finely shredded coconut, for coating

CUT Coconut Cashew Bar into about ten pieces and then pulse in a food processor for 30 seconds, or until completely broken up.

MIX all ingredients together in a small bowl with a fork until combined.

SHAPE into six bonbons and roll in a shallow dish of finely shredded coconut to coat.

FREEZE 30 minutes or refrigerate for an hour until firm.

*USE your favorite vegan protein bar and vegan chocolate for a vegan-friendly recipe.

MACRONUTRIENTS: 1 BALL PER SERVING | CALORIES: 145 | FAT: 10 G | CARB: 11 G | PROTEIN: 5 G

Morgan Buehler

DARK CHOCOLATE
ALMOND GRANOLA

SERVES: 5 to 6 | **PREP TIME:** 5 minutes | **COOK TIME:** 15 minutes

 VEGAN *option*    DAIRY FREE

Eaten alone or sprinkled atop Greek yogurt, this grain-free granola hits the spot. Got a craving for cereal? Simply pour some coconut or nut milk over a handful of this granola, and you've got yourself a high-protein, nutrient-dense treat.

- 1 cup (250 ml) almonds, chopped
- 1 cup (250 ml) cashews, chopped
- ¼ cup (60 ml) sunflower seeds
- ¼ cup (60 ml) shredded unsweetened coconut
- 1 tablespoon (15 ml) coconut oil, melted
- 2 tablespoons (30 ml) coconut butter, softened

- 1 Primal Kitchen Dark Chocolate Almond Bar* (48 g), or your favorite collagen/protein bar
- ½ teaspoon (2.5 ml) cinnamon
- A few drops stevia, honey, or sweetener of choice*
- A pinch of sea salt

PREHEAT oven to 300° F (150°C).

MIX everything except the bar together and bake until lightly golden, stirring every couple minutes.

CHOP the Dark Chocolate Almond Bar into bite-sized pieces.

ADD to golden granola and bake an additional 5 minutes.

COOL before enjoying and store in an airtight bag or container.

*USE your favorite vegan protein bar and a sweetener besides honey for a vegan-friendly recipe.

MACRONUTRIENTS: ½ CUP (125 ML) PER SERVING | CALORIES: 435 | FAT: 37 G | CARB: 19 G | PROTEIN: 13 G

VANILLA SPICE DONUTS

SERVES: 6 | **PREP TIME:** 30 minutes | **COOK TIME:** 20 minutes

 VEGAN *option*    DAIRY FREE *option*

With a faint hint of vanilla, these donuts shine with spice and are perfect any time of the day!

¾ cup (175 ml) cassava flour

2 scoops (40 g) Vanilla Coconut Primal Fuel,* or protein powder of choice

¼ cup (60 ml) date sugar plus 2 to 3 tablespoons, divided

½ teaspoon (2.5 ml) baking soda

½ teaspoon (2.5 ml) baking powder

¼ teaspoon (1.25 ml) fine sea salt

½ teaspoon (1.25 ml) cardamom

¼ teaspoon (1.25 ml) cinnamon plus 2 to 3 teaspoons, divided

4 tablespoons (60 ml) coconut oil, melted and divided

1 large egg, whisked

¾ cup (175 ml) cashew milk

1 teaspoon (5 ml) vanilla extract

PREHEAT oven to 350° F (180°C).

COMBINE cassava flour, protein powder, ¼ cup (60 ml) date sugar, baking soda, baking powder, sea salt, cardamom, and ¼ teaspoon (1.25 ml) cinnamon in a large mixing bowl.

ADD 2 tablespoons (30 ml) of melted coconut oil and stir to combine. The consistency should resemble that of little pebbles. Add whisked egg, cashew milk, and vanilla extract to the bowl, and stir to create a wet batter.

ADD whisked egg, cashew milk, and vanilla extract to the bowl, and stir to create a wet batter.

COAT a donut pan with coconut oil and fill cavities halfway with batter. Transfer the pan to the oven and bake for 20 minutes, or until a toothpick comes out clean.

WHEN you're ready to serve and the donuts are still warm, melt the coconut oil for topping. Meanwhile combine date sugar and cinnamon in a small bowl wide enough that your donut will fit.

DIP each donut in the remaining 2 tablespoons (30 ml) of melted coconut oil, and then coat the top in the cinnamon-sugar mixture. Serve warm. Store leftovers covered in the fridge.

*USE your favorite vegan or dairy-free protein powder for a vegan-friendly or dairy-free recipe.

MACRONUTRIENTS: 1 DONUT PER SERVING | CALORIES: 266 | FAT: 13 G | CARB: 26 G | PROTEIN: 6 G

CHOCOLATE PROTEIN
ICE CREAM BITES

SERVES: 8 | **PREP TIME:** 15 minutes

 VEGAN
option

 DAIRY FREE
option

These protein bites are a huge hit in our house. They're great for on-the-go snacking or as a dessert you can feel good about!

- 1 13.5-ounce can (400 ml) full-fat coconut milk, refrigerated overnight
- 1 to 2 tablespoons (15 to 30 ml) maple syrup (optional)
- ½ teaspoon (2.5 ml) vanilla extract
- 3 scoops (63 g) Chocolate Coconut Primal Fuel,* or protein powder of choice

- ½ cup (125 ml) cashew milk
- 2 tablespoons (30 ml) dark chocolate mini chocolate chips*
- 3 tablespoons (45 ml) almond butter, melted

TO make your own coconut whipped cream, refrigerate one can of full-fat coconut milk overnight. Open the can, scoop out the solid coconut cream from the top, and add to the mixing bowl. (Save the liquid for another use, like smoothies.) Using an electric mixer, whip coconut milk until light and fluffy, add in the remaining ½ teaspoon of vanilla extract and 1 to 2 tablespoons of maple syrup (if you'd like it sweeter), and whip for an additional 2 to 3 minutes.

IN a large bowl, whisk together coconut whipped cream, protein powder, and cashew milk until smooth with no lumps.

SET out eight silicone cupcake liners and evenly distribute chocolate mixture between them.

TOP ice cream bites with chocolate chips and freeze for 6 hours or overnight.

ONCE ice cream bites are frozen, drizzle with almond butter and enjoy.

*USE your favorite vegan or dairy-free protein powder and vegan or dairy-free chocolate for a vegan-friendly or dairy-free recipe.

MACRONUTRIENTS: 1 PIECE PER SERVING | CALORIES: 199 | FAT: 17 G | CARB: 9 G | PROTEIN: 6 G

ROASTED BERRY PARFAIT

SERVES: 6 | PREP TIME: 15 minutes | COOK TIME: 25 minutes

 VEGAN    DAIRY FREE   KETO *option*   NO ADDED SUGAR *option*

A bowl of fresh, ripe berries is splendid, for sure, but this parfait made from layers of roasted berries (sweet tasting like pie) and coconut whipped cream is over-the-top deliciousness.

24 ounces (680 g) fresh berries

1 tablespoon (15 ml) plus
  1 to 2 tablespoons (15 to 30 ml)
  maple syrup,* divided

2 tablespoons (30 ml) Avocado Oil

1 teaspoon (5 ml) plus ½ (2.5 ml) teaspoon
  vanilla extract, divided

Pinch of salt

1 13.5-ounce can (400 ml) full-fat coconut
  milk, refrigerated overnight

PREHEAT oven to 450° F (232° C). Line a large rimmed baking sheet with parchment paper.

IF using strawberries, hull and quarter the berries.

COMBINE the berries in a large bowl. Pour the maple syrup, avocado oil, and 1 teaspoon of vanilla extract over the berries. Add a pinch of salt and gently mix.

SPREAD the berries out evenly in one layer on the baking sheet.

ROAST 25 minutes (do not stir).

WHILE the berries are roasting, prepare the coconut whipped cream.

TO make your own coconut whipped cream, refrigerate one can of full-fat coconut milk overnight. Open the can, scoop out the solid coconut cream from the top, and add to the mixing bowl. (Save the liquid for another use, like smoothies.) Using an electric mixer, whip coconut milk until light and fluffy, add in the remaining ½ teaspoon of vanilla extract and 1 to 2 tablespoons of maple syrup (if you'd like it sweeter), and whip for an additional 2 to 3 minutes.

IN clear glasses or bowl, layer the cooled berries and coconut whipped cream.

*OMIT maple syrup for a keto-friendly and no-added-sugar recipe.

MACRONUTRIENTS: ¾ CUP PER SERVING | CALORIES: 218 | FAT: 19 G | CARB: 13 G | PROTEIN: 2 G

Adam Weston

DARK CHOCOLATE
ALMOND COOKIE MUFFINS

SERVES: 6 | PREP TIME: 20 minutes | COOK TIME: 14 minutes

DAIRY FREE
option

These treats pack the perfect texture with Dark Chocolate Almond Bar chucks in every bite.

⅝ cup (156 ml) butter or ghee,* softened

⅔ cup (150 ml) coconut palm sugar

1 teaspoon (5 ml) vanilla extract

1 ripe banana

1 Primal Kitchen Dark Chocolate Almond Bar (48 g), or your favorite collagen/protein bar

¹⁄₁₆ (0.3 ml) teaspoon baking soda

¹⁄₁₆ (0.3 ml) teaspoon baking powder

⅔ to ¾ cup (150 to 175 ml) cassava flour

3 ounces (90 g) dark chocolate* (optional)

PREHEAT oven to 350° F (180°C).

IN a stand mixer, blend butter with coconut palm sugar until creamed. Add vanilla extract and banana, then blend until incorporated. Scrape down the side of the bowl.

ADD baking soda and baking powder into the sugar mixture with the setting on low. From there, add cassava flour slowly, ⅓ of a cup (75 ml) at a time. Err on the side of the mixture being more wet than dry.

CHOP a Dark Chocolate Almond bar into small chunks and incorporate the chunks into the mix. Then lightly grease a nonstick muffin tray with butter and spoon in the batter about ¾ full. The batter will not rise like a traditional muffin.

IF using dark chocolate, add squares or shavings to the top of each cookie muffin before baking.

BAKE for about 15 minutes until the cookie muffins are golden brown. They will still be slightly gooey. Take care not to overcook them.

LET the cookie muffins cool completely in the tray. They will easily pop out once they set.

*USE ghee in place of butter and your favorite dairy-free dark chocolate for a dairy-free recipe.

MACRONUTRIENTS: 1 MUFFIN PER SERVING | CALORIES: 397 | FAT: 28 G | CARB: 38 G | PROTEIN: 4 G

CHEESECAKE
POWER BITES

SERVES: 10 | PREP TIME: 1 hour and 15 minutes | COOK TIME: 10 minutes

DAIRY FREE
option

These no-bake, two bite treats are packed with protein, gut-healing collagen, and delicious flavor! Perfect for dessert, as a post-gym snack, or even breakfast on the go! Top with berries and coconut cream to jazz them up!

10 ounces (284 g) cashews, raw whole

½ cup (125 ml) boiling water

2 tablespoons (30 ml) gelatin

1 tablespoon (15 ml) vanilla extract

2 tablespoons (30 ml) sweetener of choice

2 scoops (42 g) Chocolate Coconut Primal Fuel,* or protein powder of choice

1 tablespoon (15 ml) raw cacao powder

1 teaspoon (5 ml) coffee grounds

3 tablespoons (45 ml) coconut cream

¼ teaspoon (1.25 ml) salt

SOAK the cashews, submerged in water for at least 2 hours, until swollen and tender.

DRAIN, rinse, and place in blender.

BRING ½ cup (125 ml) of water to a boil.

ADD the rest of the ingredients to the blender.

ADD in the boiling water. Remove the cap or stopper from the blender lid. Replace the lid and cover the hole with a thick folded tea towel. Start blending on low, slowly lifting the towel to carefully vent some of the steam. After it starts to purée, you can turn up the power and blend until the mixture is thick, creamy and completely smooth. You may need to stop and scrape the mix down once or twice.

LINE a baking sheet with silicone muffin liners, or pieces of parchment paper.

DISTRIBUTE the mix, about ¼ cup (1.25 ml) in each muffin cup, which will make about ten.

SET in the fridge until firm, about an hour.

CAREFULLY peel away the muffin liners.

THESE little crustless cheesecakes will be sturdy enough to hold in your hand but creamy and smooth inside!

IF you want to create a quick crust for these bad boys and amp up the nutrition try this: In your food processor, pulse together 2 to 3 Primal Kitchen Dark Chocolate Almond Bars, or your favorite collagen/protein bar, until crumbly and sticky. Press the mixture down into the muffin liners in a thin ¼-inch (6 mm) layer before pouring in the cheesecake mix!

*USE your favorite dairy-free protein powder for a dairy-free recipe.

"Paleo isn't a historical reenactment, no one expects you to forage
for your meals (unless you want to). Paleo has evolved, it's become
this great template for optimal health, where moving often and nourishing
your body are priorities, not luxuries. Eat plants and animals.
Stay active. There are no negative side effects."

—Cristina Curp, The Castaway Kitchen

PIZOOKIE SKILLET

SERVES: 10 | **PREP TIME:** 40 minutes | **COOK TIME:** 20 minutes

DAIRY FREE
option

The perfect combination of sweet treat and protein snack— enjoy a slice with your morning coffee!

1 cup (250 ml) almond flour, finely ground

½ cup (125 ml) cassava flour

2 scoops (40 g) Vanilla Coconut Primal Fuel,* or protein powder of choice

1 teaspoon (5 ml) baking soda

½ teaspoon (2.5 ml) sea salt, finely ground

¼ cup (60 ml) plus 1 tablespoon (15 ml) melted ghee, divided

¼ cup (60 ml) maple syrup

1 egg, room temperature

1 teaspoon (5 ml) vanilla extract

2 or 3 Primal Kitchen Dark Chocolate Almond Bars (96 or 144 g), or your favorite collagen/protein bars, frozen

PREHEAT oven to 350 F (180°C) and grease a 10-inch (25 mm) cast iron skillet with 1 tablespoon (15 ml) of ghee.

COMBINE flours, protein powder, baking soda, and sea salt in a large mixing bowl. In a small bowl, combine ¼ cup (60 ml) ghee, maple syrup, egg, and vanilla. Add the wet ingredients to the dry ingredients and blend them together using a mixer. Once ingredients are well combined, refrigerate for 15 to 20 minutes, until chilled.

WHILE dough is chilling, chop up the Dark Chocolate Almond Bars into small, chip-like pieces (freezing the bars helps). Then fold the dark chocolate pieces into the dough.

EVENLY spread the dough into the greased cast iron skillet and bake for 20 minutes. (Use a toothpick to check for doneness.) Pizookie is ready when it reaches a golden color on top and a toothpick comes out clean from the center.

*USE your favorite dairy-free protein powder for a dairy-free recipe.

MACRONUTRIENTS: 1 SLICE (¹⁄₁₀ OF SKILLET) PER SERVING | CALORIES: 239 | FAT: 17 G | CARB: 13 G | PROTEIN: 9 G

DARK CHOCOLATE HUMMUS

SERVES: 5 TO 6 | PREP TIME: 20 minutes | COOK TIME: 10 minutes

DAIRY FREE
option

Chocolate fruit dip made from vegetables? Yes, you read that right! This Dark Chocolate Hummus pairs great with fresh strawberries and is 100% kid approved.

- 1 ½ to 2 cups (½ medium head) cauliflower
- 2 Primal Kitchen Dark Chocolate Almond Bars (96 g), or your favorite collagen/protein bars, softened
- ¼ cup (60 ml) almond butter
- ¼ cup (60 ml) dark chocolate chips,* melted

- 2 tablespoons (30 ml) coconut sugar
- 1 tablespoon (15 ml) cacao powder
- ½ teaspoon (2.5 ml) vanilla extract
- 4 tablespoons (60 ml) cold water, as needed
- 2 to 4 tablespoons (30 to 60 ml) Avocado Oil

BOIL cauliflower in water until tender. Once done, drain and squeeze to remove excess water. Final measurement needs to be 1 cup (250 ml) packed.

TO soften the Dark Chocolate Almond Bars, microwave for 30 seconds.

MELT chocolate chips over a double boiler. Alternatively, you can melt chips in the microwave for 1 minute to start. Remove and stir, and continue to heat at 15-second intervals until fully melted.

ADD all ingredients except the avocado oil to the food processor, and pulse until fully combined.

ADD avocado oil 1 tablespoon (15 ml) at a time until desired consistency. You're looking to achieve a smooth, thick, creamy texture. You can add more water and less oil if preferred.

TRANSFER to a bowl and chill 30 minutes before serving. Serve with fruit.

*USE your favorite dairy-free dark chocolate chips for a dairy-free recipe.

MACRONUTRIENTS: ¼ CUP PER SERVING | CALORIES: 297 | FAT: 25 G | CARB: 18 G | PROTEIN: 6 G

CAKE BARS

SERVES: 12 | PREP TIME: 10 minutes | COOK TIME: 20 minutes

DAIRY FREE
option

The original goal of this recipe was to create a protein bar, but it turned out to be so much more. While eggs and protein powder join to add loads of protein with delicious chocolate flavor, and macadamia nuts and coconut butter add lots of healthy fat, these dense, moist chocolate-coconut-macadamia bars also make a fine cake, especially when topped with whipped cream and berries. This recipe, as it turns out, is a case when you can have your cake and eat it too.

¾ cup (175 ml) coconut butter

1 cup (250 ml) raw, unsalted macadamia nuts

¼ cup (60 ml) maple syrup

½ teaspoon (2.5 ml) baking soda

¼ cup (60 ml) Chocolate Coconut Primal Fuel,* or protein powder of choice

2 eggs

¼ teaspoon (1.25 ml) salt

PREHEAT oven to 350° F (177° C).

THE coconut butter should be at room temperature or slightly warmed for a texture that is soft and runny.

IN a food processor, blend the macadamia nuts for several minutes until a smooth, thick paste or "butter" forms. (If you'd like small pieces of nuts in the final product, leave it slightly chunky.)

IN a medium bowl, whisk together the coconut butter, macadamia butter, maple syrup, baking soda, protein powder, eggs, and salt.

POUR the batter into an oiled 8 x 8-inch (20 x 20 x 5-cm) square baking dish or 8-inch (20 x 4-cm) round baking dish.

BAKE 20 minutes until the batter is set and has puffed up a bit. Let cool before cutting.

CAKE Bars can be refrigerated or kept at room temperature.

*USE your favorite dairy-free protein powder for a dairy-free recipe.

MACRONUTRIENTS: 1 SLICE (⅛ OF CAKE) PER SERVING | CALORIES: 213 | FAT: 19 G | CARB: 10 G | PROTEIN: 4 G

Ellen Jaworski

CHIA SEED PUDDING

SERVES: 1 TO 2 | **PREP TIME:** 4 hours 5 minutes

 VEGAN *option*    DAIRY FREE *option*

As someone who travels often, I know it's challenging to keep up with a healthy eating routine when on the road. So while living and working out of a hotel room, I created this simple, nutritious, protein-packed recipe to make primal travel just a little easier. This recipe requires just three ingredients: almond milk and chia seeds, both of which can be purchased at any grocery store, and of course, Primal Kitchen Vanilla Coconut Primal Fuel, which is a "must pack" in any suitcase. There's no reason to let travel cramp your primal style when you've got a simple and nutritious recipe like this!

¼ cup (60 ml) chia seeds

1 ¼ cup (310 ml) unsweetened almond milk

1 scoop (20 g) Vanilla Coconut Primal Fuel,* or protein powder of choice

1 scoop (10 g) collagen peptides* (optional)

Optional toppings: fruit, nuts, almond milk, almond butter, cacao nibs, etc.

PLACE all ingredients in a blender bottle (or any container with a lid) and shake until ingredients are evenly combined.

PLACE the bottle in the refrigerator, wait 10 minutes, and then give another couple shakes (to prevent chia seeds from clumping).

WAIT at least 4 hours, add toppings, and serve!

*OMIT collagen peptides and use your favorite vegan protein powder for a vegan-friendly recipe. Use your favorite dairy-free protein powder for a dairy-free recipe.

MACRONUTRIENTS: 1 ¼ CUPS PER SERVING | CALORIES: 204 | FAT: 5 G | CARB: 21 G | PROTEIN: 19 G

CHOCOLATE BANANA DONUTS

SERVES: 10 | **PREP TIME:** 30 minutes | **COOK TIME:** 20 minutes

DAIRY FREE
option

These donuts remind me of the classic frosted donuts that come in the white and blue package from the grocery store. When these paleo donuts are eaten cold, they taste just like I remember those donuts tasting. The only difference is that these donuts have a mildly sweet flavor, because they're sweetened with fresh mashed banana. They also have a mild chocolate flavor thanks to the protein powder.

1 cup (3 bananas) banana, mashed

1 cup (250 ml) cassava flour

2 scoops (42 g) Chocolate Coconut Primal Fuel,* or protein powder of choice

½ teaspoon (2.5 ml) baking soda

½ teaspoon (2.5 ml) baking powder

¼ teaspoon (1.25 ml) fine sea salt

2 tablespoons (30 ml) coconut oil, melted

½ cup (125 ml) unsweetened cashew milk

1 large egg, whisked

1 teaspoon (5 ml) vanilla extract

2 ounces (60 g) dark chocolate

1 tablespoon (15 ml) palm shortening

PREHEAT oven to 350° F (180°C).

MASH the bananas, measure out 1 cup, and transfer to a large mixing bowl.

ADD cassava flour, protein powder, baking soda, baking powder, and sea salt to the mashed bananas. Stir to combine until a paste forms and there are very few lumps from the banana left.

ADD melted coconut oil and stir to combine.

ADD whisked egg and cashew milk, and stir to create a more liquid batter.

OIL a 6-cavity donut pan with coconut oil. Fill each donut well halfway with batter so that the donuts will rise and not overflow. Transfer the pan to the oven and bake for 20 minutes, or until a toothpick comes out clean.

REMOVE the donut pan from the oven. Allow donuts to cool (about 10 minutes) before removing from the pan and transferring to a cooling rack. Add more batter to the pan until it's all used up.

WHEN you're ready to serve, melt the dark chocolate and palm shortening in a small pan over medium-low heat. Stir to combine. Once melted, remove from heat.

DIP each donut in the melted chocolate and transfer to a platter before serving. Store leftovers covered in the fridge.

*USE your favorite dairy-free protein powder for a dairy-free recipe.

MACRONUTRIENTS: 1 DONUT PER SERVING | CALORIES: 151 | FAT: 8 G | CARB: 12 G | PROTEIN: 4 G

"Paleo has changed my life and the lives of thousands of others. But paleo is merely the word we collectively use to describe our similar approach to wellness. Don't get caught up on the term. And don't get caught in the dogma. Learn what works best for your body and be open to making changes because nothing ever stays the same. As the Greek philosopher, Heraclitus said, *'The only thing that is constant is change.'*"

—Marla Sarris, Paleo Porn

SNICKERDOODLES

SERVES: 12 to 16 | **PREP TIME:** 15 minutes | **COOK TIME:** 10 minutes

 DAIRY FREE

These cookies are the perfect blend of chewy and crunchy. The coconut palm sugar caramelizes ever so slightly, rendering a most decadent treat. Coconut palm sugar, derived from coconut sap, may have a lower glycemic index than regular white cane sugar does, but even when consuming more naturally occurring sugar, it's best to keep the portions small. So problem solved with these Snickerdoodles, because you can have one and then share the rest with your nearest and dearest!

1 cup (250 ml) almond flour

½ cup (125 ml) plus 1 tablespoon (15 ml) coconut palm sugar, divided

½ teaspoon (2.5 ml) baking soda

⅛ teaspoon (0.625 ml) sea salt

⅓ cup (75 ml) Classic Mayo (page 13)

½ teaspoon (2.5 ml) vanilla extract

½ teaspoon (2.5 ml) cinnamon

PREHEAT oven to 330° F (166°C). Line a baking sheet with parchment paper.

ON a small plate, mix the coconut palm sugar and cinnamon, and set aside.

IN a medium bowl, mix almond flour, coconut sugar, baking soda, and salt.

IN another bowl, beat the mayo and vanilla with an electric mixer until smooth.

ADD the dry ingredients to the mayo and vanilla, and beat until combined.

USING generous teaspoon measures, shape the batter into balls, and then roll in the coconut palm sugar and cinnamon topping mixture to coat.

PLACE on a baking sheet. Do not flatten, as they will flatten during baking. Be sure to leave enough space between each cookie.

BAKE for 8 to 10 minutes. Remove from oven and allow to cool for 10 minutes before transferring to a wire rack.

MACRONUTRIENTS: 1 COOKIE PER SERVING | CALORIES: 111 | FAT: 8 G | CARB: 10 G | PROTEIN: 2 G

MEXICAN
CHOCOLATE MOUSSE

SERVES: 4 | **PREP TIME:** 15 minutes

 VEGAN
option

 DAIRY FREE
option

A guilt-free dark chocolate mousse featuring the warmth of cinnamon and chili, with healthy, satisfying fats from avocado and coconut.

2 avocados, pits removed

¼ cup (60 ml) full-fat canned
   coconut milk

1 cup (250 ml) Chocolate Coconut Primal
   Fuel,* or protein powder of choice

2 tablespoons (30 ml) raw cacao powder

1 teaspoon (5 ml) pure vanilla extract

1 teaspoon (5 ml) cinnamon

½ teaspoon (2.5 ml) ancho chili powder

Pinch sea salt

Maple syrup, to taste (optional)

Dark chocolate,* shaved for topping (optional)

PLACE all ingredients into the bowl of a food processor.

PROCESS until smooth and creamy, scraping down the sides of the bowl as needed.

TRANSFER to a serving dish. Refrigerate until ready to serve.

NOTE: Mousse will thicken slightly as it stands, so resist the urge to use less coconut milk.

*USE your favorite vegan or dairy-free protein powder and vegan or dairy-free chocolate for a vegan-friendly or dairy-free recipe.

MACRONUTRIENTS: ½ CUP PER SERVING | CALORIES: 437 | FAT: 31 G | CARB: 27 G | PROTEIN: 28 G

FROZEN COCONUT MACADAMIA BARS

SERVES: 12 to 14 | **PREP TIME:** 45 minutes | **COOK TIME:** 5 minutes

 VEGAN *option*   KETO    DAIRY FREE *option*

Is it a primal energy bar or the perfect primal dessert? Call them what you will, these delicious little morsels deliver a healthy dose of fat and protein, while satisfying your urge for something sweet. Low-calorie they are not, so don't plan on eating an entire pan of Frozen Coconut Macadamia Bars in one sitting. The good news is that the bars are so rich and satisfying that you're not likely to be tempted to overindulge. A small bar is all you need for that special occasion.

1 cup (250 ml) unsweetened flaked coconut

1 ½ cups (375 ml) raw, unsalted macadamia nuts

¾ cup (175 ml) melted coconut oil

1 to 2 scoops (20 to 40 g) Vanilla Coconut Primal Fuel,* or protein powder of choice

1 tablespoon (15 ml) chia seeds

Pinch of sea salt

PREHEAT oven to 350° F (180°C).

PUT the coconut flakes in a pan and toast in the oven until lightly browned, about 5 minutes.

LINE an 8 x 8-inch pan (20 x 20 x 5-cm) with parchment paper.

PROCESS the macadamia nuts and coconut oil in a food processor until very smooth. Add the coconut flakes, protein powder, and chia seeds, and pulse a few times.

POUR the batter into the pan. Sprinkle a pinch of sea salt on top.

FREEZE until solid, about 30 minutes.

CUT into small bars. Store in the freezer.

*USE your favorite vegan or dairy-free protein powder for a vegan-friendly or dairy-free recipe.

MACRONUTRIENTS: 1 SMALL BAR PER SERVING | CALORIES: 283 | FAT: 30 G | CARB: 5 G | PROTEIN: 3 G

CHOCOLATE MAYO CAKE

SERVES: 18 | PREP TIME: 20 minutes | COOK TIME: 45 minutes

 DAIRY FREE

Inspired by my grandmother's recipe, this Chocolate Mayo Cake is a family favorite, and it's sure to become much-loved in your own family after you make it! This cake is one of those baked goods that pleases even the fussiest of gluten-free, dairy-free naysayers—it's deliciously indulgent and perfect for your special occasions.

1 ½ cup (375 ml) fine-ground almond flour

¼ cup (60 ml) coconut flour, sifted

½ cup (125 ml) pure cocoa powder

1 teaspoon (5 ml) baking soda

¼ teaspoon (1.25 ml) sea salt

3 eggs

½ cup (125 ml) honey

½ cup (125 ml) Classic Mayo (page 13)

1 teaspoon (5 ml) vanilla

1 teaspoon (5 ml) apple cider vinegar

½ cup (125 ml) filtered water

PREHEAT oven to 325° F (160°C). Lightly grease a 9-inch (23-cm) springform pan. Line the bottom of the pan with parchment paper, cut to fit.

IN a small bowl, combine the fine-ground almond flour, sifted coconut flour, cocoa powder, baking soda, and salt.

IN a separate bowl, add eggs, honey, Classic Mayo, vanilla, and apple cider vinegar. Using an electric mixer, beat at high speed for 1 minute.

ALTERNATE combining dry ingredients and filtered water into the egg and mayo mixture. Beat to combine. You will have a nice pourable batter.

POUR batter into prepared pan and bake for 40 to 45 minutes, until set in the center.

REMOVE from oven and allow to cool for 30 minutes before removing the springform pan. Allow the cake to cool completely. Frost as desired or serve with whipped coconut cream and fresh berries.

MACRONUTRIENTS: 1 SLICE (¹⁄₁₈ OF CAKE) PER SERVING | CALORIES: 171 | FAT: 11 G | CARB: 15 G | PROTEIN: 5 G

EXTRA VIRGIN AVOCADO OIL
ICE CREAM

SERVES: 6 to 7 | PREP TIME: 20 minutes | COOK TIME: 10 minutes

 DAIRY FREE

Olive oil ice cream is great—but Extra Virgin Avocado Oil Ice Cream is otherworldly. The rich, custard-like flavor is unlike anything you've ever enjoyed. Use Primal Kitchen Extra Virgin Avocado Oil to achieve the correct flavor and stunning emerald color. The additional EVAO drizzle and flaked salt toppings are listed as optional, but they absolutely complete the extraordinary Extra Virgin Avocado Oil Ice Cream eating experience!

1 13.5 ounce (398 ml) can coconut milk

4 egg yolks

¾ cup (175 ml) Primal Kitchen Extra Virgin Avocado Oil, plus extra for topping (optional)

½ cup (125 ml) honey

½ teaspoon (2.5 ml) vanilla

¼ teaspoon (1.25 ml) salt

Flaked sea salt, for topping (optional)

HEAT coconut milk on medium heat, stirring frequently.

ADD 4 egg yolks to a medium bowl, and place the bowl on the counter next to the stove.

WHEN the coconut milk begins to steam (prior to boiling), add ½ cup (125 ml) of the hot milk to the egg yolks, and whisk.

ONCE fully whisked, slowly pour the coconut milk and egg yolk mixture into the remaining coconut milk in the pot. Continue stirring, and keep the heat low enough so that the egg doesn't cook or curdle. Cook for an additional 5 minutes until the mixture is creamy.

POUR the fully cooked coconut milk and egg yolk custard into the medium bowl, and let it cool to room temperature.

ONCE cooled, add the Extra Virgin Avocado Oil, honey, vanilla, and salt. Mix well to combine. Place the custard in the refrigerator until fully chilled.

IF you're using an ice cream maker (preferred method), pour the chilled custard into your ice cream maker and churn until it reaches your desired consistency. To make the ice cream harder, transfer into an airtight freezer-safe container until fully frozen.

IF you do not have an ice cream maker, pour the chilled custard into an airtight freezer-safe container and place in freezer. Whisk the custard every 30 minutes until fully hardened.

SCOOP ice cream into a small serving bowl, drizzle with Extra Virgin Avocado Oil, and top with flaked sea salt.

STORING ice cream: firmly press a piece of plastic wrap against the surface of the ice cream to prevent ice crystals from forming, and store in an airtight freezer-safe container in the back of your freezer. Ice cream should be eaten within 1 to 2 weeks of making—good luck keeping it longer than that!

MACRONUTRIENTS: ½ CUP SCOOP PER SERVING | CALORIES: 544 | FAT: 42 G | CARB: 45 G | PROTEIN: 3 G

"The road to wellness isn't a straight, paved path. It has twists and turns,
ups and downs, bumps and dips—but it's supposed to be this way.
You will never arrive at your exact planned destination.
Wellness is a journey. (Enjoy the ride!)"

—Leslie Klenke, *Paleo Girl*

CONTRIBUTORS

Mark Sisson is the bestselling author of *The Primal Blueprint* and one of the leading voices of the Evolutionary Health Movement. His blog, **MarksDailyApple.com**, has paved the way for primal enthusiasts to challenge conventional wisdom's diet and exercise principles and take personal responsibility for their health and well-being. Mark's efforts to promote primal living extend to a line of nutritional supplements, a book publishing company, a Primal Kitchen product line with healthy mayonnaise, salad dressing, and other functional foods, and the burgeoning Primal Kitchen Restaurants fast casual restaurant chain. Mark is a former elite endurance athlete, with a 2:18 marathon and a 4th place Hawaii Ironman finish.

Recipes: *Thousand Island Dressing*, page 29; *Simple Ketchup*, page 31; *BBQ Sauce*, page 33; *Pesto*, page 35; *Yellow Mustard*, page 37; *Dijon Mustard*, page 39; *Tartar Sauce*, page 41; *Aioli*, page 43; *Bacon Dressing*, page 45; *Fennel and Olive Omelet*, page 53; *N'Oatmeal*, page 57; *Omelet Muffins*, page 75; *Primal Scotch Eggs*, page 81; *Banh Mi Salad*, page 117; *Oyster Po' Boy Salad*, pages 121–122; *Pork Loin Salad with Date Vinaigrette*, page 125; *Crispy and Creamy Avocado Fries*, page 155; *Steak with Romesco Sauce*, page 229; *Lamb Burgers with Pistachio Pesto*, page 251; *Honey Mustard Vinaigrette Short Ribs and Radicchio Salad*, page 261; *Roasted Berry Parfait*, page 277; *Cake Bars*, page 289; *Frozen Coconut Macadamia Bars*, page 301

Jessica Beacom & Stacie Hassing are the Registered Dietitian Nutritionists behind The Real Food Dietitians website and blog. They create gluten-free and paleo-friendly recipes that are designed to be big on taste and short on ingredients, so you can spend less time in the kitchen and more time doing what you love. You can find more recipes, as well as nutrition, health, and meal planning tips on their blog The Real Food Dietitians (**therealfoodrds.com**).

Recipes: *Warm Chipotle Lime Sweet Potato Salad*, page 185; *Slow Cooker Buffalo Chicken-Stuffed Sweet Potato*, page 231; *Mexican Chocolate Mousse*, page 299

Tiffany Brande from Whole Fork has a degree in biology and has spent most of her career as a chemist. She creates healthy recipes to keep her fueled and fit. As a scientist and foodie she focuses on creating recipes made with natural foods that taste amazing at the same time. Find more of her delicious paleo recipes at **wholefork.com**.

Recipe: *Tuna-Stuffed Grilled Jalapeño Poppers*, page 131

Katie Bressack is an Integrative Nutritionist–health coach specializing in women's health, as well as a lover of avocados, smoothies, and chocolate. She works to help implement simple, healthy choices that make a big impact on women's health. She specializes in healthy weight loss, prenatal nutrition, and hormone balancing, as well as helping women reduce stress from their life to help their bodies feel confident and comfortable. Visit her at **katiebressack.com**.

Recipes: *Chicken Caesar Salad*, page 91; *Chipotle Lime Egg Salad BLT on Sweet Potato Toast*, page 94

Kelly Brozyna, the spirited personality behind the food blog **TheSpunkyCoconut.com**, began to study nutrition in 2004 when she learned that she could treat her family's health issues with diet. Free of gluten, dairy, and processed sugar, her delicious recipes are both a treat to eat and a support to optimum health. Kelly is the author of *Easy Paleo Meals*, *Dairy-Free Ice Cream*, and *The Paleo Chocolate Lovers' Cookbook*.

Recipes: *Chipotle Lime Roasted Broccoli and Cauliflower*, page 175; *Honey Mustard Chicken and Sweet Potato*, page 225

Morgan Buehler is the COO at Primal Kitchen. A Chicago-born Southern California transplant, she's obsessed with surfing, chapstick, and going to the farmers market.

Recipe: *Dark Chocolate Almond Granola*, page 271

George Bryant is a professional husband, bonus dad, and family man. He is also the *New York Times* bestselling author of *The Paleo Kitchen* and creator of the wildly popular paleo food blog Civilized Caveman Cooking Creations. After spending the first 20-something years of his life in a constant battle with his weight, and then nearly losing both his legs while on deployment as a US Marine, George took matters into his own hands and began his paleo journey. What started as a simple place to post recipes for friends has since turned into an award-winning food blog. After being in the Marines for 12 years, George has since been medically separated and is enjoying working full time creating delicious paleo recipes, while hoping to change as many lives for the better by making REAL food recipes simple and tasty.

Recipes: *Spicy Egg Salad*, page 187; *Caveman Coleslaw*, page 199

Kendra Cardoza is the founder and chef of the whole-food recipe and lifestyle blog Paleopaparazzi.com. A self-taught real-food chef, she began exploring how to heal her and her family's bodies with nutritious foods after her husband suffered a stroke and she was diagnosed with an autoimmune disease (endometriosis) in 2011. In 2013 she stumbled upon the paleo lifestyle, which sparked her passion for nutrition, recipe creation, and food photography. Kendra lives in Sacramento, California with her husband, and when they aren't cooking they love to spend their time cycling, fishing, traveling, and giving back to the community.

Recipes: *Prosciutto Mango Collard Wraps*, page 115; *Creamy Chipotle Butternut Squash Soup*, page 193

Shannah Coe is the author of the food blog My Suburban Kitchen. A consultant by day, Shannah loves spending her free time in the kitchen creating delicious, family-friendly recipes that her husband and two children can all enjoy.

Recipes: *Green Goddess Dressing*, page 27; *Spinach Dip*, page 141

Julie Crowell is the creator of FoodiesGonnaFood, a brand dedicated to flavorful and fun recipes that are good for your body and health, plus a few decadent treats to keep things interesting. Three years ago, she was inspired by a family member to dive headfirst into the paleo lifestyle, and she hasn't looked back since. The paleo lifestyle sparked a love for cooking and creating recipes that she and her family could enjoy, and Julie is now an accomplished self-taught chef. Her work has been featured in *The Washington Post* as well as *HuffPost Taste*, and she is active in the Houston food scene through the Houston Food Blogger Collective, of which she is a member. She currently lives in Houston, TX with her husband and son.

Recipes: *Pepperoni Breakfast Skillet*, page 51; *Baked Bison Meatballs*, page 133; *Honey Mustard Wings*, page 139

Cristina Curp is a Miami native with Cuban roots. She lives all over the world, following her husband's military career. As a chef and mother on the move, she's accustomed to packing up their lives (and her knives) to start over every few years. This ongoing adventure birthed her blog, The Castaway Kitchen: paleo for foodies. The blog is a collection of inventive, whole-food recipes that have helped Cristina reverse autoimmune disease, lose weight, and take control of her health and well-being. She's passionate about cooking, sharing her experiences, and enjoying life to the last drop. You can usually find her in the kitchen or on a beach somewhere.

Recipes: *"Cheesy" Zucchini Slices*, page 149; *Mustard Brussels Sprouts with Leeks*, page 207; *Mediterranean Marinated Roast*, page 245; *Cheesecake Power Bites*, pages 281–282

Vanessa Davis started the blog Plaid and Paleo to stay accountable to eating healthy a year after going paleo. It has grown into a full-blown passion, where Vanessa posts new recipes weekly. She is a lover of all things food, especially unique combinations and anything ethnic. When she isn't in the kitchen, you can find Vanessa reading a book, cheering on the KU Jayhawks, or talking about how she should probably be at a yoga class.

Recipes: *BBQ Chicken Dip*, page 159; *Buffalo Chicken Jalapeño Poppers*, page 167

Pete Evans is an internationally renowned and household chef, restaurateur, television presenter, and author, with over 10 bestselling cookbooks inspiring individuals and families in kitchens around the world. As a certified health coach with qualifications from the Institute for Integrative Nutrition, Pete wants to change the lives of everyone around him, including you.

Recipes: *Chipotle Breakfast Burrito*, pages 59–60; *Moroccan Carrot Salad*, page 189; *Pistachio-Crusted Chicken with Spicy Aioli*, pages 219–220

Alanna Figueira is the author of the e-book series *Modern Paleo Cuisine* and founder of the paleo food blog Planks, Love & Guacamole based on her love for clean eating and experimenting in the kitchen. She strives to create a sustainable paleo lifestyle for her two food-sensitive children without missing the comfort of traditional meals. Find out more about her recipes at **planksloveandguacamole.com** or on Instagram @planksloveandguacamole.

Recipe: *Chicken Pot Pie Soup with Drop Biscuits*, pages 241–242

Angelina Fracchiolla is the voice behind **jojoandeloise.com** and @jojoandeloise on Instagram. She's a wife and mother of six children (three girls and three boys). Two of her children are on the Autistic Spectrum, with the oldest one also having Autoimmune Hepatitis (a disease in which the immune system attacks and virtually destroys the liver). With different health issues and a health crisis, she has learned quickly that not all food is created equal. Quality really does matter when pursuing optimal health for you and your family.

Recipe: *Paleo Mayo Waffles*, page 67

Sarah Fragoso is a national bestselling author of six books, co-owner of JS Strength and Conditioning, co-owner of JassaFit, and founder of Everyday Paleo. Sarah is also the co-host of the popular Paleo Lifestyle and Fitness Podcast and conducts workshops and seminars nationwide on the subjects of nutrition and fitness. Her message is from the heart, and she carries a genuine desire to help other families looking for guidance. These attributes have contributed to her successes and provide the drive to keep the discoveries coming.

Recipe: *Basil Pork Burgers with Mushrooms and Basil Garlic Mayo*, page 227

Lindsay G. Freedman is a recipe developer and food photographer at The Toasted Pine Nut. She's a wife and mom to two little boys with endless amounts of energy! She loves making low-carb, gluten-free, and, most importantly, delicious food. She also loves coffee and almond butter, but that's a story for another day!

Recipe: *Zesty Tuna Wraps*, page 89

Cassy Joy Garcia has a Bachelor of Science Degree and is a nutrition consultant and an expert in the kitchen with over 400 nutritious recipes in her arsenal. She created her website **FedandFit.com** to empower healthy lifestyle transformations through clear nutrition science and delicious paleo-friendly foods. Cassy's first book, *Fed & Fit: A 28-Day Food & Fitness Plan to Jumpstart Your Life with Over 175 Squeaky-Clean Paleo Recipes*, was released summer 2016.

Recipe: *Beef Sliders with Chipotle Lime Mayo*, page 239

Natasha Gildea is a certified Nutritional Therapy Practitioner and the "feisty" recipe maker and photo taker of The Feisty Kitchen, blog and Instagram. Natasha focuses on an individualized, nutrient-dense approach to eating for health and optimal wellness. Her favorite food is anything with avocado and bacon, because FATS! When she's not in the kitchen cooking or shooting photos, she loves to be competing on the tennis court.

Recipe: *Bacon Broccoli Salad*, page 183

Valerie Grogan is a Southern California blogger at Cocos Paleo Kitchen (cocospaleokitchen.com), spreading her love of food, health, and an active lifestyle. She enjoys being creative in the kitchen, using a paleo template, and experimenting with nutrient-dense recipes. She fuels her body the way she believes our bodies were designed to eat, and therefore thrive!

Recipe: *Mini Bells as Shells Breakfast Tacos*, pages 71–72

Laird Hamilton is an American athlete, surfer, author, inventor, stunt man, model, producer, TV host, fitness and nutrition expert, husband, father, and adrenaline junkie. In addition to riding many of the biggest waves on the planet, Laird is known as the world-renowned innovator and guiding genius of crossover board sports including tow-in surfing, stand up paddle boarding, and hydrofoil boarding. In short, Laird Hamilton is the essential Water Man. Over the last decade, Laird has transcended surfing to become an international fitness icon and nutrition expert.

Recipe: *Grok on a Surfboard Smoothie*, page 83

Melissa Hartwig is a Certified Sports Nutritionist who specializes in helping people change their relationship with food and create lifelong, healthy habits. She is the co-creator of the Whole30 program, and a #1 *New York Times* bestselling author. Her books include *It Starts With Food*, *The Whole30*, *Food Freedom Forever*, and *The Whole30 Cookbook*. She lives in Salt Lake City, Utah.

Recipes: *Spicy Tuna Poke Bowls*, page 107; *Tri-Olive Dip*, page 129; *Baked Greek Salmon over Asparagus & Red Peppers*, pages 215–216; *Creamy Spiced Turmeric Chicken Thighs*, pages 253–254

Jessi Heggan grew up loving to spend time in the kitchen creating new and fun foods for friends and family, but had to rethink the way she cooked when she was diagnosed with an autoimmune disease. She turned to her kitchen for healing and began creating new and healthier recipes in the process. Jessi photographs each of her recipes and posts them on her website, **jessiskitchen.com**. She's passionate about helping people learn to cook and enjoy healthy and clean food as much as she does.

Recipes: *Chipotle Lime Cauliflower Hummus*, page 153; *Loaded Potato Wedges*, page 177

Louise Hendon is the co-founder of *Paleo Flourish Magazine* and author of the *Essential Paleo Cookbook*. She loves helping people find the biggest wins for their health—the actions and changes that will make the biggest difference with the smallest amount of effort (not just what is most popular or easiest). Louise recognizes how difficult it can be for many people to stay paleo or primal in modern life, and she helps them focus on what's important by sharing down-to-earth advice and easy-but-delicious recipes.

Recipes: *Kale and Blueberry Salad*, page 105; *Curried Chicken Salad*, page 195

Tony Horton is the wildly popular creator of the bestselling fitness series *P90X®*, *P90X2®*, *P90X3®*, and *Ten Minute Trainer®*, and most recently his 22-minute military inspired workout, *22 Minute Hard Corps®*. Tony believes that real and lasting change can happen when we commit to health as a lifestyle. Exercise, whole foods, and the right mindset is the formula that leads to a vibrant, productive, and full life for anyone who focuses on being the best they can be.

Recipe: *Spinach and Parmesan Stuffed Chicken Breast*, page 103

Ellen Jaworski, or @triplepeakpaleo on Instagram, is an art director for television, an amateur paleo recipe author, food photographer, and an active CrossFitter. She has been a dedicated member of the paleo/primal community since 2013.

Recipe: *Chia Seed Pudding*, page 291

Nan Jensen & Nicole Bangerter are the creators of the blog Whole Sisters (**whole-sisters.com**). Their focus is on creating recipes that find the perfect balance of abundant nutrition and great flavors, then sharing them with the world. Their philosophy is that eating healthy can still taste amazing!

Recipe: *Honey Mustard Salmon*, page 233

Anya Kaats is a San Diego-based blogger, health coach, and marketing consultant on a mission to share good food, health, and happiness with as many people as possible. Anya's Eats (**AnyasEats.com**) was developed out of Anya's personal health journey that continues to lead her through a lifelong struggle with digestive issues and hormonal acne to a healthy and balanced life centered around a holistic approach to health and a focus on grain-free, dairy-free, and gluten-free foods.

Recipes: *No-Rice Spicy Tuna Rolls*, pages 143–144; *Chipotle Bacon Deviled Eggs*, page 165

Megan Kelly is a Nutrition Practitioner specializing in neurobiology and quantum hormonology. Her work guides people on how to transform their body and mind through functional nutrition, mental and emotional training, and habit mastery. Megan speaks and educates on how to create a healthy fit body, an unstoppable mind, and a life full of passion and purpose. Learn more about Megan at **renewingallthings.com**

Recipe: *BLT Salad Bowl*, page 87

Leslie Klenke is the author of *Paleo Girl*, the one-and-only multi-award winning paleo book for teens and young adult women. She's also the Managing Editor for the very book you hold in your hands—*The Primal Kitchen Cookbook*—and hopes that you're enjoying these recipes as much as she does! Leslie shares her passion for good food and a healthy life on Instagram (@LeslieKlenke) and her blog leslieklenke.com.

Recipes: *Rosemary Aioli and Kaleidoscope Fries*, page 197; *Creamy Roasted Tomato Soup*, page 205; *Extra Virgin Avocado Oil Ice Cream*, pages 305–306

Chris Kresser, is the founder of Kresser Institute, the co-director of the California Center for Functional Medicine, the creator of **ChrisKresser.com**, and the *New York Times* bestselling author of *The Paleo Cure*. He is known for his in-depth research uncovering myths and misconceptions in modern medicine and providing natural health solutions with proven results. Chris was named one of the 100 most influential people in health and fitness by **Greatist.com** (along with Michelle Obama, Dr. Oz, Dr. Weil, Deepak Chopra, and Dr. Mercola), and his blog is one of the top-ranked natural health websites in the world. Chris lives in Berkeley, California with his wife and daughter.

Recipes: *French Onion Soup Gratinée*, pages 179–180; *Hazelnut-Crusted Halibut*, page 257

Marlena Kur is an innovative food blogger, recipe creator, and brand ambassador with a passion for delicious healthy meals made with clean, whole ingredients. Her love for art turns her meals into colorful plates of goodness. You can find her at **zestmylemon.com** or @zestmylemon on Instagram.

Recipes: *Chipotle Lime Salmon Salad*, page 109; *Dark Chocolate Hummus*, page 287

Kelly LeVeque of Be Well by Kelly is a holistic nutritionist, celebrity health coach, and wellness expert based in Los Angeles, California. Guided by a practical and always optimistic approach, Kelly helps clients improve their health, achieve their goals and develop sustainable habits to live a healthy and balanced life. Working with well-known names such as Jessica Alba, Evan Peters, Chelsea Handler, and Emmy Rossum, Kelly is extremely passionate about the science of human nutrition and the desire to help clients achieve their personal health goals.

Recipes: *Salmon Cakes*, page 119; *Butter Lettuce Shrimp Tacos*, page 169; *Berry Crumble*, page 265

Shannon Mann is a wife and mother with a passion for healthy cooking. With Italian and Southern roots, she formed an appreciation for the ability of food to create a bond and bring diverse people together for beautiful memories and laughter. Certain smells still invoke wonderful memories of her childhood; cooking is her love language.

Recipe: *Bacon-Wrapped Shrimp Stuffed Portabellas*, page 151

Rachel Mansfield is in her mid-twenties and living in the heart of Manhattan with her husband Jordan. In early 2015, Rachel created her Instagram (@rachlmansfield) account, followed by her blog (**rachlmansfield.com**) a few months later. Since then she has worked with the top brands in the health, fitness, food, and wellness spaces and has built a following of over 170K on Instagram. Rachel's goal and passion is to share food that not only tastes amazing, but also makes you feel amazing. Follow along as she shares her deliciously clean recipes, go-to products, favorite workouts, and lifestyle tips.

Recipes: *10-Minute Pad Thai Zoodles*, page 99; *Green Goddess Lettuce Wraps*, page 111

Janée Meadows is the author of *Lil' Grok Meets the Kings* and is the graphic designer at Primal Kitchen. Janée's artistic talents also include photography (she shot every delicious recipe you see in this cookbook), but she's best known for her throw-back style and rock-n'-roll sensibilities.

Recipes: *Duchess Sweet Potatoes*, page 203; *Coconut Cashew Bonbons*, page 269

Dana Monsees is a health and nutrition coach and the creator of the website Real Food with Dana (**realfoodwithdana.com**), where she shares recipes and nutrition tips to help you thrive with real food and a paleo lifestyle, one delicious meal at a time! Because caveman would if he could.

Recipes: *Chipotle Lime Egg Salad BLT on Sweet Potato Toast*, page 93; *Chipotle Creamed Spinach*, page 211

Ana Navarro, born in Mexico and raised in Chicago, comes from a family of chefs and restaurateurs. She found her passion for cooking while healing her hormonal condition, PCOS. She's now the co-founder of Ancer (**ancer.co**) and co-author of *Paleo MX*.

Recipes: *Cassava Flour Tortillas*, page 135; *Fish Quesadillas*, page 137

Sébastien Noël was plagued with a myriad of health issues and no answers from traditional medicine, so he began trying out different approaches to nutrition and lifestyle. This led him to explore and fall in love with the paleo and primal principles. It's from there that he decided to start a website to try and help other people, too. This is how Paleo Leap was born.

Recipes: *Zesty Greek Sweet Potatoes*, page 209; *Chicken Caesar Burgers*, page 259

Jenna Pacini is a Certified Health Coach who believes in the philosophy that we should all live life joyfully from the inside out! Follow her on Instagram for delicious recipes and inspiration @thejoyfullbelly.

Recipe: *Chipotle Avocado Chorizo Fun-Dippo*, page 147

Martine Partridge is a real, whole food enthusiast who develops and shares delicious recipes on her blog Eat Heal Thrive (www.eathealthrive.ca).

Recipes: *Snickerdoodles*, page 297; *Chocolate Mayo Cake*, page 303

Sadie Radinsky is a 15-year-old baker and lover of scrumptious, organic food. She runs the baking blog **GoodiesAgainstTheGrain.com**, where she shares her recipes for treats that are free of gluten, grains, refined sugar, soy, and dairy. Her belief is that nobody should ever feel deprived of sweets. Instead, they can make healthy treats that taste just as delicious (if not way better!) than the not-so-healthy alternatives.

Recipes: *Sweet 'n Spicy Salad*, page 101; *Double Chocolate Chunk Cookies*, page 267

Marla Sarris is an entrepreneur, educator, and cookbook author from Chicago. She runs the popular food blog **PaleoPorn.com**. After dedicating six years to teaching at one of the nation's top high schools, Marla left her career to pursue a healthier, sustainable lifestyle. She discovered paleo in 2009 and continues to indulge her passion for teaching through Paleo Porn and her cookbooks *Pigskin Paleo* and the upcoming *Paleo MX*. When she's not in the kitchen, Marla makes up one-third of SPYR, a brand development agency, and is also an Executive Producer of the feature-length documentary *Minimalism: A Documentary About the Important Things*.

Recipes: *Cassava Flour Tortillas*, page 135; *Fish Quesadillas*, page 137

Mary Shenouda, known as The Paleo Chef, is a private chef to the high performing elite across the nation for her expertise in paleo-centric, nutrient-dense, and of course, flavor-packed dishes. She is the creator of Phat Fudge, a Real Ingredient Performance Fudge, and a social media force. Her aim is to change the perception of what it means to dine with food restrictions so we can all, as her motto goes, Eat Clean, Play Often, and Crush Life.

Recipe: *Bison Chili,* pages 235–236

Amy Sheree is a self-taught photographer, food blogger, and food stylist. She runs her blog, **amysheree.com,** and Instagram, @amy.sheree, in hopes of sharing how a healthy lifestyle can not only be fun but also full of delicious food. The best part about cooking is knowing that families all over will create unforgettable memories in the kitchen, laughing, celebrating, and eating—making food even more beautiful.

Recipes: *Enchilada Sauce,* page 47; *Rise and Shine Zoodle Bowl,* page 65; *Cobb Salad Cups,* page 157; *Dill Pickle and Bacon Potato Salad,* page 191; *Chipotle Chicken Enchiladas,* pages 247–248; *Chocolate Protein Ice Cream Bites,* page 275

Chelsea Simdorn lives in Fargo, ND with her spouse and three cats. She's enthusiastic about food and CrossFit. She devotes her weekends to creating new recipes for her blog and improving her food photography skills. You can find her recipes at **DoYouEvenPaleo.net** or around the web @DoYouEvenPaleo.

Recipe: *Grilled Peach and Walnut Salad,* page 113

Charlotte Smythe, also known as Confessions of a Clean Foodie (@confessionsofacleanfoodie) on Instagram, believes that being healthy is so much more than dieting. She's passionate about giving her readers new and exciting ways to change their lifestyles, whether it's with a new recipe or a lifestyle tip. Her number one goal is to show her audience that being healthy does not have to boring. So whether she's creating a paleo, Whole30 friendly, or clean recipe, she always thinks of this journey as changing lives and NOT conforming to a new diet.

Recipe: *Coconut-Crusted Shrimp Fresh Garden Salad,* page 97

Devyn Sisson is an author, artist, culinary enthusiast, and restaurateur involved in the launch of the Primal Kitchen fast casual restaurant chain. After graduating from The New School in New York City with a degree in Psychology, she started to express her creativity with a deep immersion into the study of nutrition with the Institute for Integrative Nutrition and self-improvement through the Spiritual Psychology program at the University of Santa Monica. Devyn recently published her own cookbook *Kitchen Intuition*. She lives in Southern California where she is sort of, kind of successfully training her new dog, Ninja.

Recipes: *Grok Star Smoothie*, page 54; *Almond Spice Smoothie*, page 55; *Chia Vanilla Swirl Smoothie*, page 62; *Magenta Sunrise Smoothie*, page 63; *Thin Mint Smoothie*, page 68; *Picnic Basket Smoothie*, page 69; *Heart Beet Smoothie*, page 77; *Kale Yeah! Smoothie*, page 76; *Protein Pancakes*, page 79; *Blueberry Detox*, page 82

Kyle Sisson earned a degree in Business with a concentration in Entrepreneurship from Cal Poly San Luis Obispo. He is currently opening California's first Primal Kitchen Restaurant in Culver City alongside his sister Devyn. Kyle hopes to make clean eating and healthy living more widely accessible through the spread of Primal Kitchen Restaurants.

Recipes: *Grok Star Smoothie*, page 54; *Almond Spice Smoothie*, page 55; *Chia Vanilla Swirl Smoothie*, page 62; *Magenta Sunrise Smoothie*, page 63; *Thin Mint Smoothie*, page 68; *Picnic Basket Smoothie*, page 69; *Heart Beet Smoothie*, page 77; *Kale Yeah! Smoothie*, page 76; *Blueberry Detox*, page 82

Barb Taft is the creator of the paleo-inspired recipes blog **PrimalDish.com**. She started following a primal/paleo diet in 2012 and the change in lifestyle transformed her health. A long-time fan of cooking, Barb began creating paleo recipes and sharing them on social media. She enjoys coming up with new flavor combinations to fuel her growing six-year-old triplets and her previously paleo-phobic husband.

Recipe: *Pizookie Skillet*, page 285

Tina Turbin is a renowned author and a celiac and gluten-free advocate. She researches and writes about the benefits of the gluten-free, paleo-ish, keto, and lower-carb-inclined diets while also supporting and promoting the ethical companies she believes in. Tina's award-winning site PaleOmazing (**PaleOmazing.com**) houses many of her multi-award-winning recipes and research articles.

Recipe: *Marinated Filet Mignons*, page 223

Vevian Vozmediano was born in Baghdad, Iraq, spent most of her life in Detroit, and is now living in Los Angeles. She started a project "January 2013" where she offered to live with families and teach them how to cook healthy recipes tailored to their family's wants and needs. Since then, she has lived with 52 families around the world and has worked with over 100 across the U.S. She also has 12 eCookbooks and has recently started a family meal prep service.

Recipe: *Veggie Sushi*, pages 161–162

Adam Weston started his early food interest while cooking at age five with his mother and her friends amidst the many ethnic families in the area. The seeds of love of the original, no recipe, creative dishes were planted early in Adam. He courted Julia Child and Jacques Pepin from his living room, learning techniques and experimenting with whatever his mom had in the fridge. Flash forward 45 years and not much has changed, except the ingredients. Adam and his Primal Health Coach wife Kelly (**imfitandhappy.com**) inspire friends and clients with primal-centric, original dishes, helping them discover healthy eating. Adam is a foodie to the heart and soul; every day is a tasty and healthy adventure.

Recipe: *Dark Chocolate Almond Cookie Muffins*, page 279

Robb Wolf is a former research biochemist, health expert, and author of the *New York Times* bestseller *The Paleo Solution*. He has been a review editor for the *Journal of Nutrition and Metabolism* and *Journal of Evolutionary Health*, serves on the board of directors of Specialty Health Medical Clinic in Reno, Nevada, and is a consultant for the Naval Special Warfare Resilience Program. Wolf is also a former California State powerlifting champion and holds the rank of blue belt in Brazilian Jiu-Jitsu. He lives in Reno, Nevada with his wife Nicki and daughters Zoe and Sagan.

Recipe: *Sunchoke Salad*, page 173

Index

EAT LIKE
YOUR LIFE
DEPENDS ON IT

MAYOS & AVOCADO OILS

| Mayo | Chipotle Lime Mayo | Egg-Free Mayo | California Extra Virgin Avocado Oil | High Heat Avocado Oil |

DRESSINGS, VINAIGRETTES & MARINADES

| Greek Vinaigrette | Ranch Dressing | Honey Mustard Vinaigrette | Green Goddess Dressing | Caesar Dressing |

GRASS-FED COLLAGEN PROTEIN BARS

| Dark Chocolate Almond | Chocolate Hazelnut | Macadamia Sea Salt | Coconut Cashew |

COLLAGEN FUEL™

Chocolate Coconut   Vanilla Coconut

visit us at primalkitchen.com